Lights, Cameras, Lions is a fascinating story of a man whose career involved the training and care of exotic species, particularly animals used in motion pictures, television and live animal shows. However, the book is much more; it is a tale of a young man who escaped the oppression of Cold War-era Hungary and created a successful, unique, and gratifying career in America. Yes, this is the classical immigrant story, but in Hubert's case, the work he chose to do has been mastered by relatively few. His personal biography alone makes a good read, but the details of his animal subjects and what they did is gripping. As a veterinarian, I knew many of the book's characters, both human and animal, so it was meaningful to me, but I believe most readers will be moved by the incidents and individuals so dramatically portrayed in this narrative.

– Robert M Miller, DVM, author of *Yes, We Treat Aardvarks: Stories of an Extraordinary Veterinary Practice* and *Understanding the Ancient Secrets of the Horse's Mind.*

In a wildly entertaining saga that takes us behind the scenes of Hollywood's animal kingdom, Hubert Geza Wells delivers an unforgettable, irresistible true tale set in a world rarely visited. With self-effacing humor and vivid details, Wells brings to life his nearly four decades as one of the most in-demand animal trainers in the movie industry. Navigating what he calls the euphoric heights and infernal lows of this little-known profession, he takes us from his roots training animals in Europe to coaching his non-human stars to hold their own alongside the likes of Meryl Streep, Robert Redford, and Carol Burnett. Working in movies and television and live on stage across five continents with a multitude of animal thespians—from ants to elephants, but specializing in lions and birds of prey— the author more than earns the title of Real-Life Dr. Doolittle. The magical moments of uncanny communication between Wells and his animal actors make this fascinating memoir a must-read for those who love animals, movies, and great stories well-told.

– Mim Eichner Rivas, author of *Beautiful Jim Key: The Lost History of a Horse and a Man Who Changed the World*

T0098541

Lights, Camera, Lions

"The difficulty as you rake over the coals of memories, is which one to lift in the tong of remembrance."
— The Earl of Portsmouth

Lights, Camera,
LIONS

MEMOIRS OF A REAL-LIFE DR. DOLITTLE

HUBERT GEZA WELLS

NEW YORK

NASHVILLE • MELBOURNE • VANCOUVER

Lights, Camera, **LIONS**
MEMOIRS OF A REAL-LIFE DR. DOOLITTLE

Published in New York, New York, by Morgan James Publishing. Morgan James is a trademark of Morgan James, LLC. www.MorganJamesPublishing.com

The Morgan James Speakers Group can bring authors to your live event. For more information or to book an event visit The Morgan James Speakers Group at www.TheMorganJamesSpeakersGroup.com.

ISBN 9781683500995 paperback
ISBN 9781683501015 eBook
ISBN 9781683501008 hardcover
Library of Congress Control Number: 2016908557

Cover Design by:
Chris Treccani
www.3dogdesign.net

Interior Design by:
Chris Treccani
www.3dogdesign.net

In an effort to support local communities, raise awareness and funds, Morgan James Publishing donates a percentage of all book sales for the life of each book to Habitat for Humanity Peninsula and Greater Williamsburg.

Get involved today! Visit
www.MorganJamesBuilds.com

Dedicated to Doree, who for the last seven long years has shared with me the euphoric heights and infernal lows in the life of an animal trainer.

I'd like to thank all of my fellow trainers, friends, and competition. First of all, Cheryl Shawver, who was my right hand on many productions, Jules, whom I found in Africa, pulling a snake out of the ground, Cowboy Paul, who took the cover and last but not least, Cynthia Maxwell, who's diligence and patience helped to make this book a reality.

PREFACE

I am an endangered species, a living fossil, a walking dinosaur. For 45 years I trained birds and beasts for the motion picture industry. I started my career in the last century in Hungary, the country that gave us Zsa Zsa Gabor, Count Dracula, and the national dish Goulash. In 1956 after the Russians crushed our bloody uprising against Bolshevism, I defected to the West and ended up in the Eastern U.S.A.

Eight years later I moved to California with my Indian Leopard and golden pointer. A job awaited us, a two part T.V. show for the Disney Studios.

In the following years my animals, and at times, myself, as a stunt double appeared in over 150 films, T.V. shows and commercials.

My animals received seven PATSY awards (Performing Animal Star of the Year). My lions are in the Oscar winning film, "Out of Africa".

Movie training is different from any other form of animal handling. In the circus, the trainer is in a steel cage with his group of predators. In the movies, I was responsible for a large crew and exotic humans like Rex Harrison, Robert Redford, Meryl Streep, Elizabeth Taylor, and Pee Wee Herman. In Africa, Jackie Kennedy stepped out of a hot air balloon to pose with my lioness playing the role of Elsa in the "Born Free" series.

On the triple Razzies Award winning film "Sheena Queen of the Jungle" I took 5 lions, 3 leopards, 4 chimpanzees, 4 white horses, 1 Rhodesian Ridgeback,

12 flamingos, 2 macaws, 1 elephant and 1 rhino to Kenya. A world record for animals shipped back the cradle of mankind.

Sheena was a bad picture, almost painful to watch, but for me and my crew it was fun to do and financially rewarding.

What I have done with real animals future generations will only read about. Digitally created, cheesy wolves in the "Twilight Saga" and ridiculous C.G.I. lion in "Narnia" are replacing live animal actors.

In my book "Lights, Camera, Lions", I bring the past alive, not to lecture, but to entertain.

CONTENTS

Preface   xi

Chapter 1   Is This Any Way To Make A Living?   1

Chapter 2   Permit Me To Introduce Myself: 1934–1945   7

Chapter 3   But It's Only 1945, Mr. Orwell: 1945–1954   21

Chapter 4   The Hills Are Alive With The Sound
             Of Filming: 1954–1956   29

Chapter 5   Seven Days Of Freedom   45

Chapter 6   Welcome To Vienna   57

Chapter 7   "Give Me Your Poor, Downtrodden, And Confused"
             1957–1964   67

Chapter 8   Hooray For Hollywood: Also For Burbank   89

Chapter 9   Once There Was A Place Called Jungleland   97

Chapter 10   To The Island Of Droon Or Otterely Ridiculous   111

Chapter 11   Ladies And Gentlemen, This Is Our Last Performance   117

Chapter 12   There Is No Business Like Monkey Business   119

Chapter 13   Kwa-Heri Means "So Long"   131

Chapter 14   *Hawmps* Or Ride Them Camels, Cowboys   161

Chapter 15   M'Zee Simba, The Old Lion   165

Chapter 16   *Sea Gypsies* And *Wilderness Family*   169

Chapter 17   *Rasing Daisy Rothschild* Or *The Last Giraffe*   173

Chapter 18   Never Cry "Wolf," But Beware Of The Director   177

Chapter 19   *Sheena, Queen Of The Jungle*, And Five Raspberry Awards 183

Chapter 20   The Sundance Kid In Africa   189

Chapter 21   Out Of Africa Into The Frying Pan   195

Chapter 22   The Clan Of Seven Producers And One Lonely Cave Bear   203

Chapter 23   Ivory Coast, Land Of Bad Ju-Ju   207

Chapter 24   The Man-Eaters Of *Ghost And Darkness*   *211*

Chapter 25   Angkor Watt, But What For? Or Tiger,
              Tiger Burning Bright   221

Chapter 26   Bits And Pieces   231

Epilogue   The Age Of Stone Lions   239

About The Author   245

CHAPTER 1

IS THIS ANY WAY TO MAKE A LIVING?

CALIFORNIA 1968

Candy wasn't large or especially fierce, as tigers go. She was an average striped cat, but she was irritated by the torrid Santa Ana winds and at me. I was trying to teach her to sit on a pedestal. As she stood on her hind legs, her mouth, studded with three-inch serrated fangs, hovered a good foot above my face. Her pupils wide open, two craters of green lava. Her bark, the most frightening sound an animal can make, exploded from the depths of her resentful diaphragm. No other animal sounds like an angry tiger. It's as unnerving as the hiss of a grenade landing at your feet. I knew someone was about to get hurt. I knew it was going to be me.

She lashed out with a forceful right. Then she was on top of me, and we both fell to the sawdust floor. I must have raised my left arm to cover my face. A sharp numbing sensation shot through the fleshy part of my palm. There was no pain; I knew more by the crunching sound of muscle and the warm fluid running down my wrist that I had been bitten. No, my whole life did not flash before my eyes. But as I was lying there, pinned down by 300 pounds of vindictive cat, the thought occurred to me: "Is this any way to make a living?"

FLORIDA 1963

I had been presenting my dog-and-leopard act in St. Petersburg. Webb's City is a sprawling complex of specialty stores covering two city blocks. With good reason, Webb's City calls itself "the largest drugstore in the world."

I had just returned to the hotel after the day's final show. The desk clerk was waving frantically, "Two reporters have been looking for you all day, Mr. Wells. Reporters from *Life* magazine. They want to do a story about you and your animals."

The next day, we took Lolita and Amber for a frolic by the Silver River. Lolita, a full-grown leopard, and Amber, a yellow retriever, romped through the Florida jungle like inseparable friends. The *Life* photographer and writer were amazed. And they were right to be. In the wild, a leopard will do almost anything to nab its favorite delicacy—a dog.

The photo spreads appeared a few weeks later when I was back in New York. Lorraine D'Essen, owner of this city's largest animal agency, and an accomplished author, was impressed. With a touch of envy in her voice, she remarked, "I suppose you bought up all the copies in Manhattan."

"No," I told her modestly, "I only bought a dozen. I'm sure you would buy at least that many if one of your animals appeared in *Life*."

I was proud. I'd achieved a long-standing ambition—to be in *Life*, the most prestigious magazine in the world.

Is this any way to make a living? You bet your family album it is.

HOLLYWOOD 1987

An aging game show host is being interviewed on a TV gossip show. His wavy hair is silver with a touch of blue. Until recently, it was chestnut brown. He had discovered, to his horror, that the hair dye he used contained "animal products." His sensitive conscience was so outraged that he went silver almost overnight.

His eyes burn with the conviction of a judge at the Spanish Inquisition as he reveals the deep, dark secrets of the Hollywood animal trainers. His host seems outraged. She asks more questions with well-rehearsed spontaneity. They don't mention me by name, but the industry knows full well that the villain of this story is me.

I had just finished one of the most demanding projects of my career, working a large group of chimpanzees. Despite the difficulties, we pulled it off without an injury to man or animal. But here I was, being hauled over hot coals in the media, and a criminal action hanging over my head like the sword of Damocles. Nobody seemed interested in hearing our side—least of all this self-appointed Inquisitor of Trainers.

During this ordeal, I continually asked myself, "Is this any way to make a living?" On days like this, certainly not.

KENYA 1974

Evening in Maasai-Mara. My Land Rover is clanking along the winding trails of one of the last strongholds of wildlife on this overcrowded planet. I am lying contentedly on the jolting roof. A good day's filming is behind us. There is peace in my soul and before my eyes is indescribable beauty.

Beside me is a tawny film star. Her name is Asali, which means "Honey" in Swahili. She's classically proportioned—a lioness in her prime. Her amber eyes reflect the riotous tropical sunset. Flared nostrils filter the myriad scents of the bush. I know she enjoys the magic of the evening as much as I do. There is a kinship between us, one that stretches back through the ages to the caveman who coaxed the first wolf to his campfire. Is this any way to make a living? You bet your last Kenyan shilling it is.

AFRICA 1984

A sawed-off giant of a studio executive stands before me. Only five-foot-two in his elevator shoes, but he thinks he can look down on me from the exalted position of power. He wants to hire marksmen with high-powered rifles to cover my lions when I work with them.

"I insist on using sharpshooters every time a lion is on set," he says. "Robert Redford's life is worth more than your lions."

The short hairs on my neck are bristling; a spring of anger winds tighter in my stomach. But the safety catch is on. I am not going to lose it. My voice turns a shade softer, the volume a half a decibel lower. The giant of the industry has to step closer to hear me. He looks directly at my Adam's apple.

"That's not the point, sir. The life of the last beggar on the streets of Nairobi is worth more than all my lions together. I fully realize that. And I do take elaborate precautions. But having a loaded gun on the set will never be one of them.

Be logical. When would the sharpshooter practice his craft? When the lion is approaching the camera? That's what the scene calls for. And what if, God forbid, the worst should happen and the lion knocks someone down? If your William Tell blazes away, then he could kill or injure the man or further infuriate the animal. This is not the first time I've turned a big cat loose on a movie set. Like Indiana Jones said: 'Trust me.'"

The issue was closed. The sharpshooters never materialized, and we filmed all the scenes without bending a hair on Robert Redford's head. That's how it often is in this business. Nobody would think to tell the cameraman, or even a grip, how to do his job. But somehow everyone thinks they know how to be an animal trainer. Not only that, but they think they can do it better. When I have to fight that kind of ignorance and often just plain concentrated stupidity, I ask myself: Is this any way to make a living?

HOLLYWOOD 1986

The light slowly dims on the ornate ceiling of a movie theater. The mood of the music changes. Now it has subtle undertones of lurking menace. You can feel the tension running through the audience. The actress is clinging to the bole of an acacia tree, as if she'd like to disappear into it. Then Asali, the most beautiful lioness that ever lived, steps from behind a thorn bush.

This is the first of the four lion sequences in the Oscar-winning film *Out of Africa*. The scene never fails in its magic, no matter how many times you see it. Drawn by the magnet of a defenseless human, the big cat approaches. I know she will hit her mark like the old pro she is, but even I can't help a faint uneasiness:

"What if she keeps on coming?" She freezes, lifts her head, her gaze settling in the general direction of Meryl Streep's throat.

I have seen it a dozen times, and at this moment I always hear the audience catch its breath. The magic of the movies is working, as it should. And Asali, my trainers, and I are all part of it. Is this any way to make a living? At moments like this, you bet your last donation to the World Wildlife Fund. Of course, it is.

———————

I have trained animals for forty-five years. The list is practically endless—literally from aardvarks to zebras. I have taken lions to the Serengeti, wolves to the Arctic tundra, chimpanzees to the African jungle. I have water-skied with elephants, skin-dived with sea lions, sidestepped charging Cape buffalo. I have sweated in the 125-degree heat of Lake Rudolph, shivered in a record-breaking 86-below-zero in Alaska. I have also worked with some of the world's most exotic humans, including Sophia Loren, Robert Redford, and Elizabeth Taylor.

I have been charged by rhino and bitten by snakes. My skin is tattooed with scars donated by every big cat except the jaguar. It's been a hair-raising but healthy life. I am close to 60 now, and I am still ready to wrestle lions, tigers, or giant snakes whenever the script calls for it.

All over the world, wild animals have been pushed to the brink of extinction. The same can be said of the animal trainers. Training exotic animals for the camera is a demanding and complicated profession. In recent years, it has become more difficult, thanks to misguided efforts of the lunatic fringe of the Animal Protection Industry. Slanderous attacks, innuendo, senseless regulations, and, sometimes, pure malice have made animal trainers an endangered species.

The future for us does not look bright. But I have survived a world war, a bloody revolution, and 200 stitches, so perhaps this new danger will pass too.

Over the years I have collected a rich store of memories. At times, I have been supremely happy, at other times so miserable I felt like dying. This book is my memoir of a life in an unusual profession. I hope the reader will find this glimpse into the world of the professional animal trainer enlightening, but mostly entertaining.

How did it all begin? How does one become a first-generation animal trainer? No one is born with high boots, riding britches, and a chair in one hand. At least I wasn't. It started as a hobby that slowly but surely got out of hand. It began so far away and such a long time ago I could almost say "Once upon a time . . ."

CHAPTER 2

PERMIT ME TO INTRODUCE MYSELF

1934–1945

I hail from a land of knights and wandering gypsies. From the country that gave us Count Dracula, goulash, and Zsa Zsa Gabor. It's a small country in Eastern Europe, about the size of Delaware, called Hungary. Geographically, it is situated in a corridor, where East meets West. The conquering hordes of Mongols, Tartars, Turks, and Slavs always had to trample through Hungary to get at Western civilization. And trample they did.

Hungary is ringed by an ocean of Slavic peoples, but Hungarians are not Slavs. We call ourselves Magyars. Scientists tell us that the Hungarian language and Finnish are somehow related, but so are the elephant and the hyrax, a rabbit-sized African mammal. It's hard for the layman to see the connection.

Legend has it that a tribe of seven clans came from the steppes beyond the Ural Mountains. They were led by two princes, Hunor and Magor, who were chasing a golden stag. By the time they had reached the basin of the Carpathian Mountains, the stag vanished. At this point, history takes over from legend. The Magyars saw that the fertile basin would make a great place to settle. A slight problem—the land was already occupied by Slavs. But a Magyar chief named Arpad offered the locals a beautiful white stallion in exchange for "a handful of earth, a sheaf of grass, and a jug of water." The Slavs jumped at the deal. Only then did they discover that Arpad had been speaking figuratively. They had unwittingly sold their land, rivers and grazing. They objected, naturally, but they were no match for the hardened nomads from the Asian steppes.

The Magyars conquered the Slavs, but the wandering, looting lifestyle was hard to give up cold-turkey. So for a couple of centuries, when bored, the Magyars mounted their shaggy little ponies and—with their Asian-style curved bows and unorthodox combat style (fighting dirty)—terrorized the Teutonic princedoms, fiefdoms, and duchies of the West.

For a century, the litanies of the pious Teutons included the following prayer:

PRIEST
De sagittis Hungarorum salve nos, Domine.
(From the arrows of the Hungarians save us, O Lord.)

CHOIR
Amen.

All good things come to an end, and so did this reckless period of pillaging. In the late 900s, our first king, named Stefan the First (aptly), adopted Christianity as the official state religion. Stefan sent out foreign missionaries, and, unlike his forefathers, he preferred to use gentle persuasion. When that failed, as in the case of a few recalcitrant pagan chieftains, he simply buried them alive. He did such a thorough job of spreading the faith that Pope Sylvester the First rewarded him with a golden crown. After his death, he became Hungary's first saint.

Then followed a few centuries of more or less glorious kings—some sinners, some saints. In the 1500s, the Turkish Empire began looking for more space. The Turks defeated Hungary at the battle of Mohacs in 1563, and since then we won almost every battle, but unlike the English, we never won a war.

In the early 1940s, as history records, the following conversation occurred between Franklin Delano Roosevelt and his aide-de-camp.

ENTER aide-de-camp (ADC), morning papers in hand.

ADC: Good morning, Mr. President. Today Hungary declared war on the United States.

FDR: Hungary? Where the hell is that exactly? Fill me in a bit, will you?

ADC: Well, sir, Hungary is considered a Balkan country, but it is not on the Balkan Peninsula. It's a kingdom, but it has no king. Its regent, Admiral Horthy, is a seaman, but he has no sea. Shall I continue?

FDR: No, thank you. I think I got the picture.

But let's not get ahead of history. In the 1930s there was still peace, and the proverbial "good old days" were in full swing.

My father, Karl, was a forest engineer. He served on the enormous estate of the rich Count Nicholas L—. Being a forest engineer is a particularly European profession, a combination of forester and gamekeeper. Father planted saplings, supervised tree harvesting, organized the annual hunt, and was responsible for all the wild creatures of the forest. That part interested me most. I was going to follow in Dad's footsteps.

I was given the name Hubert after the patron saint of woodsmen and hunters. I've never forgiven Pope Paul I for dropping Hubert from the list of canonized saints, but luckily, I received two other saintly names—Laszlo and Paul—plus the pagan name Geza, for good measure.

Karl and the Count were good buddies. They would often leave the saplings, foxes, and bunnies behind and disappear into the jungles of the capital: the sparkling city of Budapest. Being rich, the Count could well afford the good life. He had his own gypsy band, drank imported champagne, and entertained a long procession of perky dancing girls. Years later, after the war, the Count lost everything and became a boiler cleaner. My father, who always insisted on paying his own, was less able to pay for these amusements. He got deeper and deeper in debt, until one day, when I was about four, he hocked my Mum's silver (a family heirloom), gassed up his savannah-yellow BMW, and disappeared into Austria. He was the first member of our family to defect to the West but not the last. My only memory of my Dad is a live ram he gave me for my fourth birthday. It came with a red leather harness, hooked up to my baby carriage: my first act in show business.

We relocated in the western part of the country, the rolling hills of Transdanubia, where my Mum's family owned some fertile land, good green pasture, vineyards, and acres and acres of forest. Our new home was an old whitewashed brick house with a red tile roof and a carved wooden porch.

My father had gone, but I did not grow up like a weed. My mother saw to that, and she had the help of four other guardians. They were my uncles, Josef the Strict and Paul the Handsome; my saintly Aunt Clara the Good; and, holding us all together with gentle but very strong hands, my dear Grandma, Irma the Firm.

My grandmother was a bone fide baroness, although she never used her title. Later I came to view her as combining the qualities of Scarlett O'Hara and Karen Blixen. She was decisive, forceful, inventive, realistic, and kind. Looking back, I see how well she personified the times between the two wars in Hungary. Grandmother Irma would have been at home in Margaret Mitchell's Old South, and she would have been an outstanding figure among the early settlers of British East Africa.

Between the wars in Hungary was a time and style of living one can only glimpse today in a Strauss operetta. We were the last beneficiaries of Europe's waning feudal system. We had the best of the system, of course, living the life of the landed gentry. We had no slaves, but we did have peasants: sharecroppers, herdsmen, coachmen, and gamekeepers. My playmates were their sons, but mostly their daughters. For some reason, my personal gang consisted of six girls, all older than me. I was easy to tell apart by my better clothes and cleaner face, but the sign that often gave me away was my shoes. Unlike the village kids, I was never allowed to run barefoot before the end of May.

Family Portrait, peaceful life in 1938

For years I was the only child in the family. So naturally all the adults in the family practiced pedagogy on me. Paul the Handsome instructed me in gymnastics, as if I needed more exercise. He was also a fountain of knowledge about nature. Clara the Good spoiled me rotten. Josef the Strict wanted me to work. "Go help pick the apples," he would say, or, "Come with me. I'll show you the difference between wheat and rye." And before I could escape, it was, "Now go and help slop the hogs."

Josef was tall, lean, with a high forehead and a Transylvanian edge to his face. Although he had a sarcastic sense of humor, life was no joke to him. I wasn't expected to turn in long hours, but he wanted me to acquire some discipline "to prepare you for real life." I resented every second I couldn't spend roaming the hills and woods with my gang. I never dared tell Josef what I was thinking: "Why should I work? Grandma is rich, and anyway we have the peasants." I was petrified of him, although he never struck me. "If I ever hit you," he warned, "you'll remember it when your short and curlies turn gray."

It was mostly his look and voice that kept me in check. At the sound of his stentorian bellow, even our prize bull, Mephisto, cowered in his stall. Next to Josef, I respected—hell, let's be honest, feared—this bovine gentleman the most. He had been imported from Switzerland, and he was the E. F. Hutton of the barnyard. When he growled, everyone listened. At watering time, three herdsmen led him to the long trough—one by the ring in his nose and two hanging on to ropes cross-tied to his sharp, stubby horns. During this twice-a-day ceremony, I was never allowed to leave the safety of the fenced yard, and for once I gladly obeyed the grownups.

Every season had its own charm. The main event of spring was the return of migrant birds from mysterious southern lands. The black and white wagtails were the earliest pilgrims to arrive. The first swallows began to arrive in April. In Eastern Europe, swallows are considered God's birds no matter how much of a mess they make. Every year, they nested under the eaves of the porch, and one year a couple raised their young in a mud nest clamped to the wall above our kitchen stove. No one ever thought about disturbing them. Aunt Clara told me a story about a bad boy who was horrid enough to poke a hole in a swallow's nest, and the next day all the cows in the village had blood in their milk. I believed every word of it.

My favorite birds were the elegant white storks. A pair nested on our chimney every year. I would watch for hours their dignified comings and goings, trying to catch them at their main job: the delivering of babies. Government grants for nature research were non-existent then, but it might be a good idea to assign a few millions of the taxpayers' money to find out exactly how these birds do it. And what about when the storks went to Africa? I never got a satisfying answer to the riddle of winter babies either.

Most of July and August we spent at my grandmother's villa on the shore of Lake Balaton. This is one of the biggest lakes in Europe, a shallow, reedy expanse that we affectionately called the Hungarian Ocean. Here I explored the secrets of a strange, watery world. For a young boy already in love with nature, it was a paradise.

The trip took about three hours by train, but most of the supplies were sent ahead by a small caravan of horse-drawn wagons. Old Siggi, my favorite coachman, was the leader of this expedition. His weather-beaten face could have been painted by Rembrandt. He had the long whiskers of a catfish, and in his leather brown neck the wrinkles were chiseled x-shape, instead of horizontal. The four coaches carried baskets of fruit, clothing, sheets, pillows, and eggs packaged tightly in newspapers. And hanging from the tailgate, in crates woven by gypsies from pliant twigs of willow, traveled dozens of sacrificial chickens and ducks.

It was my life's unrealized ambition to make this trip with Siggi instead of in a stupid, smelly train. No matter how much I nagged, my request was never granted. Even Clara the Good was against me. "What would happen to you if it rained? The drivers sleep at night under the wagons in a pile of straw. You'd hate that. No. It's out of the question."

I would have loved to sleep under the wagons in a pile of straw. Couldn't these heartless grownups see that was exactly the special attraction of the journey? Year after year, I watched Siggi take his seat, twirl his heroic moustache a couple of times as he winked at me. "See you at the lake, young master." He cracked his long whip over the team of grays, and I stood there broken hearted and watched them go until there was nothing but a plume of dust like a derisive gray finger mocking me on the horizon.

The lake had many new varieties of fish and frogs to discover. But I needed a boat to explore the wilderness of the reeds. The family boat was too big and clumsy. Not to worry, between washes I confiscated the wooden washtub from Nancy, our long-suffering maid. The tub was a masterpiece of gypsy carving, made of willow, and for paddles I used my palms. For hours I would wind my way through the narrow alleys of the weed labyrinth, gazing into the secret lives of wild ducks in their velvet plumage.

I learned patience from the herons as they stood snake-eyed and motionless, waiting for silvery fish. And once I was convinced I saw a parrot. It was a smallish bird, with feathers of cinnamon red and sparkling turquoise. I was disappointed when Paul the Handsome, who was an expert at these things, explained to me, "There are no parrots in Europe. What you saw was an ordinary kingfisher." Ordinary, my foot.

I caught frogs, snakes, tadpoles, and finger-sized bream, with their red dorsal fins and tails. The same Nancy who kept losing the washtub was also our cook during the summer months, and she had to fry my prized breams. They had more bone than meat, but I felt like a provider. And for a serious supper there was always chicken or roast duck.

In September we returned to the old homestead. The long-whitewashed house waited for me, solid and unchanging, security itself. The house was the cornerstone of my carefree childhood. I assumed it would be there forever, like the land and the woods that surrounded it. From the sunlit porch yawned a cavernous hallway. On its arched ceiling was a fresco symbolizing the four seasons. The old house had lots of treasures. In the parlor, in an aged walnut case, a grandfather clock measured time. Its shining brass pendulum was a unicorn ridden by Diana or some other naked goddess. Both Diana and her steed held great fascination for me.

Our village, like most villages then, had no electricity. A family evening by candlelight, or by the warm glow of the kerosene lamp, is etched deeply on my growing soul. I would fall asleep watching the shadows of the antler collection on the wall and imagine that phantom stags were re-fighting old battles in the flickering light. I did not mind the trophies on the wall, but I was decidedly wary of the Boo. The Boo was a huge oil painting of a stag, portrayed at the height of mating season. I can still see every hair of his powerful body. His front legs stiffly planted on the carpet of crushed autumn leaves, and his thick, black neck thrown back in defiance. Proudly, he trumpets his challenge to unseen rivals. Hot breath curls from his throat, and the misty-eyed cows of his harem look timidly at their lord and master. If I had to pass by him alone on a twilight fall or winter evening, I would always hug the opposite wall. Once by candlelight I swear I saw his head move.

Around the house stretched the endless garden. Two pine trees at the entrance were so tall that the winter stars seemed to rest on their tips. This was my terrain for long games of highwaymen and gendarmes, cowboys and Indians, Tarzan and peasants, mysterious home of many imagined jungle beasts. In the middle sprawled an ancient wild chestnut tree. Spring covered it with candelabras of white and yellow flowers. In the fall, the brown and white fruit, when peeled from the resisting spiky hull, would become currency to trade for marbles, slingshots, bits and pieces of string, and other items that we all had to have. The real curiosity of this tree was that it provided a home for a clan of gnomes. The best kind. Similar to Santa Claus' elves, these little people manufactured toys and, from time to time, left one for me on a thick limb. It must have been the old clan of elves that used to leave toys for my mom, aunt, and uncles when they were young. Clara even heard them discuss which toy to leave. "This and that, and that and this—that's what the head elf said. "

Late in October was the grape harvest. The marvels of technology were not for us. Everything was done by man- and woman-power and teams of patient oxen. In the vineyard was a weather-beaten old building—not really a house, though, in a pinch, one could spend a night on its moldering horsehair couch— where the new wine was made. The door was solid oak. Embedded in it was a ball of lead, fired at my grandfather's chest by a frustrated highwayman half a century earlier. Most of this building was taken up by a great press, carved from wood and assembled without a single nail. The centerpiece of this machine was a giant wooden screw, which was turned by a team of men. The first pressing of the grapes was by bare-footed peasants. The screw was used to squeeze the last drops from the trampled grapes.

The nearest town was 20 miles or two hours by horse and buggy. That's where I first saw electric light, a toy store, and my first movie. It was an early Johnny Weissmuller epic. From then on, my fantasies expanded to new horizons. Our garden became the African jungle. Stray cats became lions and leopards but never tigers. Due to the expertise of Paul the Handsome, I knew that tigers only lived in India.

In the winter, we went to town by a sleigh, and the horses were harnessed with silver bells. The frost settled on old Siggi's moustache and bushy eyebrows, and I was toasty under a blanket of black wolf furs, just like a Russian movie— Tsarist times, of course. Had history not interfered, I would probably still be living in our quiet village. My experience of Hollywood would have remained confined to celluloid fantasies. But history did interfere. In the late 1930s the grownups started to talk about "the atmosphere of war."

Next to nature, I was always fascinated by books. My mother noticed this interest and used to keep me indoors in bad weather. She also taught me to read long before school age. When I wasn't doing damage outdoors, I'd curl up before the blazing fire and take imaginary journeys with the help of pictures and the printed word. Uncle Paul had an extensive collection about travel and hunting in far-off lands. One of them was titled *The Land of Elephants*. It was an easy-to-read diary-style description of a hunting/collecting safari by one of our aristocrats. Even more than the Tarzan movie, this book was responsible for my infection with the Africa bug.

I did not want to be a forest engineer anymore. Too tame for me. I decided I would be a hunter of lions when I grew up. So far, I had seen these big cats in print only, but in the summer of 1939, I met the King of Beasts face-to-face. The zoo in Budapest was an old establishment then, hopelessly outdated by today's standards, but even today the buildings glow with an antique charm. The entrance is built like the façade of a Hindu temple; under the arches stand four gray elephants carved in stone. Between their colossal feet, mahouts crouch in the lotus position of yogi. All the zoo buildings are impressive, but the elephant, rhino, and hippo exhibits are palatial. They are tiled with green copper, and animal-head gargoyles snarl from the gutters.

The big cats were housed in an artificial mountain the size of a city block. The outdoor runs opened from the bowels of this man-made range. At feeding time, the animals were lured deep inside the mountain, where they were caged in a long, narrow cavern. This tunnel was open to the public, but not to be recommended to cat-haters and claustrophobics. Only a low guardrail and a row of iron bars separated visiting humans from beasts.

Naturally, I insisted that we stay until feeding time. Inside the tunnel, the smell of ammonia, a characteristic byproduct of old zoos, brought tears to my eyes. I didn't mind. I stood mesmerized by the proximity of so much power and beauty. Keepers wheeled out the carts of red meat, and then all hell broke loose. There must have been twenty lions, and at the sight and smell of food, all turned into snarling, spitting demons. The keepers, equipped with two-pronged iron forks, would spear a dripping chunk of meat and throw it on a narrow ledge before the cats. Flopping on their sides, the frenzied lions would reach out, claws extended. No insurance company would tolerate a method of feeding like this today. It was a barbaric excitement straight out of Roman times.

The attendants reached the end of the line when the biggest black-maned lion started to roar. He sucked the ammoniac air into his lungs. His flanks narrowed with the effort as the rolling sounds of thunder reverberated from his throat. His brothers in adjoining cages took up his challenge with answering roars. In the narrow space, the effect and volume was like standing next to a jet fighter in a wind tunnel. The spirit of adventure left me. My knees started to knock. I grabbed Clara's dress with clammy fingers and dragged her outside. My first sentence after I regained my hearing and speech became a proverb in the family: "I don't think we have enough money to send me to hunt lions anyway."

Later, in 1939, the war broke out. In our library there was a heavy book. On its dark blue cover, embossed in gold, was an eagle spreading his wings, holding a double-edged claymore in his talons. It was the history of the First World War, or, as it was then called, the Great War or "The war to end all wars." On a full-page illustration was a fallen cavalryman, buried under his horse. The bandage on his head was soaked with blood; panic and unbearable pain were in his expression as he reached up to his distant companions for help. The impact of this image was so profound on my young mind that I had to find protection from the terror of it. "It's only a drawing," I told myself. "It's not a photograph. Nothing in real life can be as horrible as this." I was wrong, of course. The dying cavalryman was romanticized, and real death was anything but romantic.

One morning in 1942, I woke up to the incessant rumbling of heavy carts, the neighing of horses, and the metallic clang of motorized war wagons. I looked out of the window. Our yard was overflowing with German soldiers. At this stage of the war, Hitler had given Hungary two choices that amounted to no choice at all: either fight on Germany's side and risk being killed by Russian bullets later, or we'll crush you right now. Once, Hungary was tied to her geographical fate. However unwillingly, we were forced to join the fight on the side of the loser.

The Germans began drafting Hungarians. Uncle Paul was one of the first. In November he left by train for the Russian front. He was my grandmother's favorite child. She tried to pull strings to exempt him or at least delay his departure. He would hear none of it. His patriotic fever burning high, he was off to fight, as he said, "The red menace, the hordes of godless Bolsheviks." We received three pink postcards from him, sent from somewhere near the Dneipir River in Russia. Then one evening a very strange thing happened. We were sitting at dinner when Paul's zither, which was kept on top of the wardrobe, exploded. All the strings snapped at once with a noise like an angel shot to earth. A fourth pink postcard arrived with a carefree message in Paul's handwriting, but by then he was already dead.

Paul had been on a scouting mission for his artillery when a Russian cannon scored a direct hit on him and his horse. There wasn't enough left for burial. I missed him then as a child, and sometimes I still miss him. Our interests were the same. We loved animals and the woods and fields. We would have become good pals. I can still picture him jumping hurdles on his bay gelding or flirting with the peasant girls at harvest time. Paul Sebastian, in the prime of his life, twenty-four and young forever.

The war stayed at a manageable distance for a while. Joseph and Clara married their sweethearts. Clara's wedding was probably the biggest event the village ever saw. It was springtime and blossoms from the chestnut trees lined the road from the old house to the church. I had the honor of carrying Clara's train. My first pair of long pants itched. The Monsignor droned on and on as I stood there with tears in my eyes. Not because I was moved but because my tight new shoes were maiming my toes.

Step by step, the war rolled closer. In June 1943, the Russian army was in and by December 1943, they would be crossing the Carpathians. We all knew it was just a matter of time. We still spent our summer weeks at the lakeshore. Only now the air was filled with the constant drone of engines as waves of British and American bombers flew over. Now and then, Messerschmitt fighter planes harassed them. The noise of the dogfights shattered the air above the lake. AK shells exploded and drifted like white dandelion puffs. One morning, I was out in my floating washtub when I caught a glimpse of something dark bobbing up and down in the waves. I rowed closer. It looked like the curved mouth of a large catfish. I reached under with the oar, lifting it partially out of the water. It was a flier's mitten. With or without the hand, I never knew. I dropped it in a hurry and rowed away as fast as I could.

In 1943 I saw the first Americans. Dogfights took place over the land as well, and the white flowers of parachutes floated slowly down to earth. A group of excited villagers surrounded the downed airmen like a swarm of hornets. The most belligerent, the village shoemaker with the club-foot, shook his pitchfork at the pale, frightened faces. At this crucial moment, Grandma arrived on the scene. One withering look from her and the mob dispersed like hyenas at the arrival of a lioness. She put a bandage on an injured head and spoke some reassuring words in French. Shortly after, the German MPs arrived and took the fliers away.

The sounds of battle came closer every day. Then suddenly the Germans were gone. The uneasy quiet lasted only hours. On a mild spring morning in March 1945, the Russians arrived. T34 tanks churned up the street. Although the family rule was "no bare feet before May," I took off my shoes, rubbed some mud on my pants, and blended in with the rest of the kids. We watched the infantry march into town. In contrast to the dapper Teutons, the Russians looked shabby and smelled bad. With the enlisted men, it was just dirt. The officers smelled worse because they doused themselves in suffocating patchouli cologne.

A group of Russian officers took over the house, letting us keep the smallest room. A wire antenna stretched from the chimney to the big chestnut tree, and the radioman shouted the words "Kochetka, kochetka. Yatanyetz, yatanyetz." Up to this day, I don't know what the words meant, but I can't shake them from my memory. We all learned another Russian phrase quickly enough: "Davay chas!" It means, "Give me your watch!"

CHAPTER 3

BUT IT'S ONLY 1945, MR. ORWELL

1945–1954

P eace broke out. We were officially liberated. Nobody felt optimistic. "A war we can handle" was the joke. "But please, not another liberation." The Russians stayed, retreating to barracks scattered at strategic locations. We didn't see much of them, but there was no doubt they had the power and pulled the strings.

I finished four years of elementary school, and it was time to start my higher education in town. I was handed over, body and soul, to the priests—a teaching order known as the Piarists, the Fathers of St. Vincent.

The Communists took control gradually. Within six months, they confiscated most of the land. It was the law that each person could keep one hundred acres.

Irma figured all her children were entitled to a hundred acres each. Somehow, she convinced the commissars of that, so we kept four hundred acres—still a good bit of land. I still had my gangs of village chums, and my main interest shifted to birds of prey. Once again I fell under the influence of a book, *The Winged Masters of the Chase*. Black and white photos of hawks, eagles, and falcons in training and action. There was very little technical information in the text, but the pictures alone were enough to start my lifelong passion for falconry.

Once, during my long wanderings in the woods, I spotted a goshawk's nest. Getting up to it presented a major problem. The tree was a grizzled old giant, the first limb at least thirty feet from the ground. The trunk was thick, smooth as satin, un-climbable. Even my friend Pete thought it was impossible, and he was the best climber in the district. But there is more than one way to scale a tree.

In a dark, dusty corner of the church loft, we found a thick rope. It was once attached to the largest bell, taken out of the church at the beginning of the war to be melted down for weapons. I didn't exactly steal the rope. In the nave was a statue of St. Anthony of Padua. I left a handful of change in the collection box for him. St. Anthony looked at me with his puzzled smile, but he didn't interfere.

The sporting goods store in town had among its collection, and only God knows why, a pair of giant barbed fishhooks. It's still a mystery to me why in, a landlocked country, one could find hooks big enough to catch the granddaddy of great white sharks. The salesman was curious as to why I need them. My explanation, that I was going to catch a young hawk with them, left him even more puzzled.

We wired both hooks securely to the end of the rope. The rest was relatively easy. Pete and I hot footed it back to the forest. The parent birds raised all kinds of fuss around us—a good sign that there must be a youngster in the nest. I tied a light string to the end of a heavy rope and a small stone to the end of the string. With my slingshot I fired the stone over the limb, and the loose end fell within my reach. Cautiously, we dragged the rope with the monster fishhooks up to the branch. One forceful yank and the hooks grabbed the limb.

The nest had three fuzz-covered nestlings. The middle-sized one was soon in the shirt of my acrobatic friend. I had taken my first important step in becoming a professional. Joseph the Strict didn't think so. His first look at the hungry, screeching bird almost gave him a coronary. "Don't you think it's time you grew up a little? What a waste of time. This is not the Middle Ages. You'll never make a living fooling around with birds." But I was stubborn, and against all opposition I kept the bird. He grew bigger and stronger every day. At the end of summer vacation, I took him with me to school, to the consternation of the good Fathers.

I called the bird Fulgur, Latin for "lightning." Maybe my choice of name impressed the Fathers a little. They let me keep him. Fulgur was, after all, a perfect name for this lightning fast predator. I have always been careful to pick distinguished names for my animals and birds. I would never call a lioness "Elsa" or a wolf "Fang."

Fulgur, my first Goshawk

Fulgur lost his white fuzz and sprouted steely gray-brown feathers. It was time to get some serious falconry equipment. In an attic, I found a patchy old motorcycle glove. It became my gauntlet. I carved jesses from soft calfskin leather and attached them to the bird's yellow shanks. We would take long excursions before and after classes. Goshawks have one unpleasant habit. Falconers call it "slicing." In layman's terms, it means the forceful ejection of feces. The chalky white waste can cover a distance of up to ten feet. We used to take bets on how far the next slice would splatter.

Fulgur wasn't housebroken—no bird ever is—but in a bus or train he would restrain himself for hours. Of course, the first slice after these trips were record breaking. He was deadly around dark suits and dresses. I stepped off a bus once, and Fulgur's messy missile scored a bull's-eye on a lady's navy blue dress. It was on her back, so she didn't notice, but Fulgur and I beat a hasty retreat.

By late fall, he was a fully-grown hunting bird. Our walks took us further and further from town. With very little prompting, he learned to follow free. At the edge of the forest, I would cast him to the top of the first tree. He followed as I walked on, hopping and gliding from branch to branch. If I startled a pheasant into flight, Fulgur was in a perfect position to swoop on it. At the end of the day, at the sound of my whistle or the sight of my extended motorcycle gauntlet, he would kick away from the tallest tree and land smack on my fist.

There's something in that impact, when the bird returns to your hand, that is the essence of falconry. It confirms the invisible, intangible bond between man and this wild bird. Even when the bird is hovering on the edge of a cloud or perched on the highest tree, I can feel the bond. It is a physical and mental symbiosis, a strong yet unforced and unenforceable link between two beings. A bit like being in love.

The bond between the Hungarian people and their leaders was an entirely different affair at this time. Hungarians, they may have been, technically, but their ties were with Moscow. On the political and economic front, the screws of oppression tightened year after year. By 1949, the state had taken over all education. The good, gentle Fathers were now "class enemies." On a dark and ominous night, they vanished. They were herded into cattle cars and shipped away to exile in isolated villages in the east.

A year after the Fathers had gone, we received an official notice. Our land had been in our family for a couple of centuries, and it no longer belonged to us; the state now owned it all. The long white house where I spent so many happy years would become a cinema for the people. No compensation, no appeals, no questions. We had forty-eight hours to get out.

Joseph and Clara had gone with their families to Budapest. They melted into the unanimity and relative protection of the big city. We had only one place to go. Somehow the commissars had overlooked our summer home, the villa at the lake. It was a charming place to be in the summer, but never meant to be a year-round dwelling. There were wood-stoves in the kitchen and the bedroom. The rest of the house in the winter was like Siberia. The wind cut mercilessly across the lake. My mom, Irma, and I found refuge there.

I released Fulgur in a part of the forest that abounded with game. I fed him well, cut the jesses from his bright yellow legs, and cast him to a distant tree. His orange eyes glared at me as I slipped away like a traitor. He didn't follow. It was getting dark, and he was full. That was the last time I had a crying jag that lasted for hours. I had to let Fulgur go. I couldn't afford the small amount of meat it took to keep him.

I finished the last years of high school by commuting five hours every day by train.

The 1950s were one of the darkest periods of history in Eastern Europe. Our Soviet masters dropped all pretense of democracy or multi-party rule. There was only one power: the hammer and the sickle. They called this a classless state, but all they did was turn the social structure on its head. There were now four official classes. From the top down, they were Workers, Peasants, Intelligentsia, and Class X. In school, we were classified by what our parents' social class had been before the invasion. My family belonged to the despised former landowners, exploiters of the downtrodden peasants. That put me neatly in Class X; in official speak, I was a "class alien."

With a stigma like this, it was hopeless to try for higher education. I went through some motions. I applied to an agricultural college and to my Dad's alma mater, the University of Forestry and Mining in Sopron. I received no answer, not even a rejection slip. I found work on a road building crew. Throughout the summer of 1952, I pulled tree stumps from heavy clay, pushed wheelbarrows, slashed cement bags, and dumped them into the swirling tank of the road building machine. At the end of the day, I was as gray as an elephant. My ears, nose, and hair held enough cement to fortify a small bunker.

In the late fall, the road work came to a halt. I had no choice but to live with Josef and Clara in the big city. I found Budapest, the city that glittered so brightly in my imagination, to be drab and overcrowded. But people lived in it somehow. My plan was to apply for a position at the zoo. Monkey keeper, bird feeder, bear cleaner, anything just to be near animals again. Josef the Strict vetoed these efforts. He hammered me with the same good, sensible arguments as before. "Wake up to reality, and learn an honest profession." Grandma always took my side in our arguments, but this time, Josef won.

Josef was now a semi-skilled laborer at a construction plant. This was his first manual labor job. He was proud of the way he stood on his own with the born proletariat. And he had connections. So I ended up with a job at a machinery repair plant. I swept the shop floor and delivered new parts to the mechanics. I spent hours scrubbing caked oil off of compressors, bulldozers, and pile drivers.

I had only known one or two communists in my home village; country folk by and large ignored the new official philosophy. They were too smart to buy the opiate of the workers' paradise. I expected the industrial labor force in Budapest to be different. If they weren't true red, surely, they'd be at least a deep shade of pink. Yet these simple true sons of the proletariat hated the very word communism.

Someone said it is impossible to govern at the point of bayonets: not true. How else could a handful of Russian puppets subjugate a nation of ten million? They did it with thousands of Russian soldiers and tanks behind them and a ruthless army of secret police to watch us. The Hungarian version of the KGB was the AVH, loosely translated as the "Authority for the Defense of the State." Years later, I read George Orwell's *1984* and *Animal Farm*. These volumes sum up better than anything why a perfect dictatorship works and will keep on working in its creaky, shoddy, insensitive fashion indefinitely, as long as the ruling class is determined to hang on to power. The saying was then: "There is only one true communist in the country, but you have to be very careful—no one knows who he is."

We knew who he was in our shop: the local party secretary. Heated political discussions all came to an end when he entered the work shed. There was nothing cynical about this man's devotion. He must have loved the system. The rest of us hated it. We were constantly coerced into singing the praises of our oppressors: the cause of all of our misery, the occupying Russians. It's humiliating enough to live under foreign domination, but the most painful part of slavery is to be forced to kiss the boot that is pushing your head into the dirt.

For a year I got up every morning like a robot and took the tram to my workplace. I scoured the slimy parts of oily monsters until the pores of my skin had sludge deposits like thousands of tiny blackheads. I was miserable. But I knew there was nothing unique about my predicament. Many people all over the world, in every social system, get up mornings and travel to and fro to a job they don't really care about. The big difference is that free people always have the chance to break out of the rut. In my dreary factory job, I was without hope, like one of Dante's condemned.

Being a melancholy Eastern European, the thought of ending it all (at the ripe old age of nineteen) haunted the periphery of my thoughts. Maybe it was never a serious thought, more like extreme self-pity and a kind of safety valve. The "undiscovered country" is oddly appealing to the adolescent mind. The thought that you don't have to go on forever. Nirvana, the black sea of nothingness at your disposal; all it takes is a firm decision.

A year later I lost my factory job. That piddling, low-paying, floor-sweeping, oil-washing job. And in a worker's paradise, where there was no unemployment, I was unemployed. There was a slump in construction; fewer machines needed repair, and naturally the janitor is first to go.

CHAPTER 4

THE HILLS ARE ALIVE WITH THE SOUND OF FILMING

1954–1956

I took the train to the villa by the lake. The vast expanse of water reflected the clouds, changing its mood with the wind. It was late spring. The place was lonely, and I took long walks on the beach. I had no idea what I was going to do. My only prospect was another soul-crushing factory job. My dream of working with animals seemed impossible, as distant as the clouds towering above the lake. Then a letter came from Auntie Clara in Budapest. With it was a newspaper clipping about Steven R.K., the man who wrote *Winged Masters of the Chase.* By this time he had become a successful nature photographer. With several short documentaries and two full-length features behind him, he was embarking on a new animal film. Titled *Pals*, it would be the story of two dogs and a bird of prey—a goshawk just like my Fulgur.

Grandmother Irma, who always protected my eccentric habits, galvanized all concerned into action. The assistant production manager of the crew, Uncle Laci, was a friend of the family, a hunting companion of Paul and Josef from the good old days. There must have been hundreds of idealistic youngsters in the country who wanted to work with R.K., but I had a foot in the door . . . a small foot, but a foot just the same. Letters went back and forth. The sun came out in its full glory. Life was once more worth living, and happiness was my middle name. I got an interview with the great R.K., and I had my first job on a film crew.

Official goshawk trainer was still beyond my reach—there was no opening in the animal department—but they made me camera assistant to the big man, R.K. himself. He was a doctor of law who had switched to photography and filming. His greatest talent was an unbending willpower to achieve and create. He wrote the scripts and shot every foot of his films. We had to call him Comrade Director, not because he was a party member with any left-leaning tendencies, but because the title commanded respect. He insisted on respect.

I soon met the rest of the small crew. The chief animal trainer was a quiet, wiry man named Adam. He became my instructor, mentor, and father figure. Meeting him for the first time on a forest trail was like meeting Saint Francis of Assisi. Two dogs and a wolf romped ahead of him, while behind snuffled a wild boar, a pine marten, and a badger. In the treetops, a tame goshawk followed his every move. Adam's affinity with animals was virtually miraculous. I am sure it had something to do with his self-confidence and his enormous physical strength. Animals respond to body language, and his confidence communicated itself to them. One day I saw Adam scale an eight-foot-high fence to separate two fighting red deer stags. They were both twelve pointers at the height of their powers. Seizing the aggressor by the antlers, Adam flipped him on his side. The stag was temporarily demoralized. He regained his confidence in a few days, however, and threw his rival over the same eight-foot fence.

Before becoming a trainer, Adam had studied to be an agriculturalist. I soon discovered that on this show only the animals were exactly what they seemed. Even my Uncle Laci, the production manager, was originally a lawyer. He was renowned as a chain-smoker, joke-smith, and a connoisseur of gypsy music. The assistant bird- and dog-man was Alex, a lad of my own age. The son of a farmer and harness maker, he had the natural intelligence of a badger and the strength of a young bear. He was also the only known specimen of the Eastern European Packrat. His formal education consisted of three years of elementary school, two and a half of which he spent as a truant, roaming hill and dale in search of objects for his collection. He collected anything that caught his fancy—birds' eggs, butterflies, unusual pebbles, even oddly shaped twigs. His interests were very like my own. I collected things too, though I was never in the same league as Alex. The only female crew member was Eva, the assistant director. She was tall, blonde, vivacious, Junoesque, sophisticated, energetic, and sensuous. She was also the wife of Comrade Director and therefore tragically unapproachable. Quite a crew indeed.

The two dog stars of *Pals* were Gossip, a black and tan dachshund, and Chum, who was a Hungarian breed called Vizsla. Of all the breeds of dog I have worked with, the Vizsla is my favorite. Almost all of them are remarkably beautiful and versatile. They are the only sporting dog that combines the virtues of the pointer and the retriever. The breed was developed by the ancient, sporting Magyar noblemen, one of whom started the first Vizsla studbook in 900 A.D.

Chum was a perfect specimen. One look at his fine rusty-gold physique told you he was an aristocrat. More than that, he was a star. Working with Chum was such a fulfilling experience that I have never been without one Vizsla or another from that day since. Given the chance, Chum would have followed me to the ends of the earth. Three years later, his daughter would do almost exactly that.

The stars of Pals, Chum, Gossip and Nimrod

The story of *Pals* was suggested by a book, *Lassie Finds a Way*. A rural gamekeeper sends his two dogs and his trained goshawk to a fair by plane. The plane develops engine trouble, and the crew jettisons most of the cargo, considerately enough attaching parachutes to the animals' crates. The Vizsla lands on the shore of a lake. He chews his way to freedom. Nimrod, the goshawk, is the luckiest. A branch tears a gash on the canvas side of his crate. He hops out and flies free. Gossip is not so fortunate. She parachutes into a lake, where she sinks to the bottom in her heavy crate. Her friend, the Vizsla, rushes to her aid. Swimming like a canine Johnny Weissmuller, he follows the bubbles and dives six feet down to the sandy bottom. He grabs the handle of the crate in his powerful jaws and then fights his way back to the shore. The pals are reunited, but they are on their own in a strange land. Their master is hundreds of miles away, but the dogs and the hawk take a bearing on the invisible compass built into the brain of some lost animals, and start the long journey home.

Chum dives to save his friend Gossip

Years later the Disney studio bought the film. At first the idea was to keep it on the shelf, out of competition with the recently released, very similar *Incredible Journey*. But some of the footage was so spectacular, and the animal action so exciting, that it was judged too good just to collect dust. An edited, English-narrated version played several times on the Disney channel as the *Legend of Two Gypsy Dogs*.

Filming started a few miles east of Lake Balaton in one of the largest swamps in Europe. We set up on a small, reedy island. The scenery was Biblical. A deep river meanders through shallow lakes. Its stagnant side branches are home to otters, muskrat, catfish, carp, and millions of birds. Our temporary home was the Island of Cormorants, where generations of nosy fishing birds nest in the ancient, lightning-scarred willows.

The air was thick with millions of hungry mosquitoes. And the water offered no sanctuary. We were constantly being attacked by legions of leeches. We were being eaten alive by the slimy bloodsuckers, and we complained bitterly. Comrade Director became so irritated with our complaints that he forbade us to use the word "leech." Once, Alex climbed out of the water with dozens of the black parasites sticking to his body. Being within earshot of the director, he moaned, "Damn, these beetles are biting the shit out of me." Daily, we slapped our bodies with guaranteed mosquito repellant imported from Sweden. Maybe it worked on the Swedish mosquito. Our Hungarian insects seemed to be using it to sharpen their syringes. Although the mosquitoes were undaunted, we did discover that it kept the leeches at bay.

The tangle of reeds stretches as far as the eye can see. Flat-bottomed boats specially adapted to marsh navigation are the main mode of transportation. The entire area was designated as a major reserve; even now, is strictly closed to the public. Our guide, Gabor, was a local poacher turned gamekeeper. He knew every inch of this wild, watery kingdom. He rowed his flat-bottomed boat stern first as he balanced precariously in the prow. He used a single long oar—a gondolier of the swamps. Most fishermen of the region couldn't swim a lick, and Gabor was no exception. Once, he told us how he got drunk at a wedding and, on the way home, lost his usual rock-steady balance. The river there was narrow and deep, and the current was powerful.

"Then what happened, Uncle Gabor?" we prompted breathlessly.

"Well, I just walked on the bottom until I grabbed the root of a willow and dragged myself out. Even drunk, I had sense enough to walk sideways, not lengthwise."

For the main animal parts, we had four Vizslas, four dachshunds, and six hawks. Adam and Alex were occupied with their care. I helped whenever I could get away from my duties as an assistant cameraman to Comrade Director. It wasn't often enough. For weeks, Comrade Director would film the nesting cormorants. The grips built a portable film tower made from sections of hardwood, bolts, and prayers. Some of those towers rose to a height of eighty feet. They were as dangerous as they looked. Perched at the nauseatingly high top of a tower was a blind. Week after week, Comrade Director would crouch in this four-by-four canvas cube and film the family life of fishing birds. My duties were to prepare the collection of lenses, maintain the motor of the French-made cameflex, brush out the cassettes, load raw stock in the magazines, and, on demand, hand an object—lens, battery, light meter, etc.—to Comrade Director with speed, haste, and alacrity. He called me a "little fox terrier" because I was twice as fast as his previous assistant, which was still about 400 percent too slow.

Adam's recreation was fishing. A rod and reel was too easy for him. He was an expert on all sorts of arcane and obscure methods for catching fish, and this was the ideal terrain to try them all: fish traps made of reed, complicated labyrinths where fish found their way in but not out, throw nets to use in the shallows, nets stretched between two poles and held against the uneven mud bank of the river, or just reaching into holes with bare hands and arresting fish by the gill. After a successful catch, the reward was a spicy native bouillabaisse. Eva was the master chef. The result wasn't just any fish soup. It was a ceremony, a ritual handed down from ancestors who lived off the land. Naturally, it had to be cooked outdoors in a copper kettle. For many recipes, one had to have at least four kinds of fish—carp, pike, catfish, and bream—onions fried to golden brown, lots of red peppers, and, to make it perfect, the fire had to be built with cherry wood.

Comrade Director took his filming very seriously. The motto "it's only a movie" wasn't in his dictionary. He didn't spare himself or us. I didn't mind a bit. After the soul-killing drudgery of the factory, this was a dream life indeed. We had no lunch breaks. We had breakfast and a lunch/dinner combination at the end of the day. Meal penalty was unheard of.

My biggest responsibility was loading magazines. Film was imported and expensive. Improper loading might cause a jam, and the gears could chew up the sprockets; we could lose a scene that was impossible to recreate. The cassettes had to be loaded in complete darkness. Eva was my instructor. The tiny darkroom was crowded. Shelves and the enlarging table made it difficult to move around. The darkness was also filled with Eva's perfume. I was aware of every rustle of her clothing, every accidental touch of her body. There was hardly enough room for one man, let alone a young, horny man and a beautiful woman. The girls in my high school and the lasses of the village were just that: girls. Eva was a woman—in every sense of the word. She was eight years older than I, mature, passionate. In a short while, I was her captive.

I thought I was playing it very cool, the lucky page picked as her knight. Our cassette-loading sessions became longer and longer. The rest of the crew began to look at me a bit strangely. The darkroom was cramped, and the impatient Comrade Director could easily bust down the door, but I lived for the wild necking and groping in the dark. I had become the toy of a passionate, playful, and desirable woman. I couldn't think of a better fate. I almost died when I once tasted cigarette smoke on her breath. She didn't smoke. The only smokers in the crew were Adam and Uncle Laci. So just minutes before joining me in the darkroom she must have been kissing one of them—but which one?

A few days later the crew took an evening off. We went by boat to the nearest town. Comrade Director stayed in his cottage, working on endless rewrites of the script. Our group ended up at the inn. There was a gypsy band and a roaring fire. Like ranch hands at the end of a long trail ride, the crew took to the local wine and rum with more enthusiasm than wisdom. I drank little; mostly, I was watching Eva. When she danced with Adam I knew whose smoke I had detected on her lips.

Adam was drinking wine with rum chasers. By midnight, he was biting chunks out of his glass and swallowing them. There were tears in his eyes. His lips were bloody.

"Have you ever been in love, Hubert?" he asked.

"Maybe," I said, glancing at Eva. I managed to take the broken glass from his hand.

"Don't worry about it. You see? Glass can't hurt me. A woman, that's what really cuts you to pieces."

Eva seemed to be sobering up fast. Adam's glass-eating performance had not impressed her. Even with my inexperienced eyes, I could see that their affair was over. I saw how a strong man can let a woman reduce him to the level of a carnival performer. It should have been a lesson to me, but it wasn't.

The next day we were expecting visitors from film headquarters. Eva went to gather flowers for the guest room. I went with her—I wanted to use the opportunity to put an end to our affair. The setting was ideal for a bittersweet parting. In the lovely solitude of still water and whispering reeds, we filled the boat with yellow water lilies. In the middle of the lake there was a thatched hut, and there I told her we were through. No arguments, it's only the right thing to do. She pulled me close for a final kiss. The kiss went on and on. We made love till sunset. Oh well, breaking off wasn't such a good idea anyway. I'll never forget that thatched hut in the lake. Years later I saw a picture of it in a coffee table book. It was called *The Natural Treasures of Hungary*. The photographer didn't know the half of it.

The filming of *Pals* went on and on. The footage pleased the executives back in Budapest, but we were far from finished. Winter was setting in. Some days the wind and rain made it impossible to shoot. At the end of November, we packed up the equipment, the dogs, and the birds and moved to winter quarters. We would be in hiatus until next May. I went to Comrade Director and asked to be transferred to the animal department. He was reluctant to lose me as a camera assistant—a higher position than animal trainer, after all—but he saw how determined I was. So at the end of my first season, I became an assistant animal trainer.

Our company was located twenty-five miles east of Budapest in a former royal park. Alex and I were in charge, and Adam would supervise us occasionally. We discussed Eva once as we walked the animals. He never mentioned her again. Alex had a fiancée in his hometown who was driving him bananas. A letter from her took days to read and digest and at least a week to answer. Every letter from her he saved in a fancy carved box with a heart-shaped lock. I helped write his replies. Alex was so lovesick he once tried to open the lock with a burning match.

"Hey, what are you trying to do?" I asked him as he poked the flame at the lock. He turned red as a lobster. He probably thought he had taken a key out of his pocket instead of a match. Or, subconsciously, he hoped to melt her frozen heart.

He stammered, embarrassed and defensive, "Someday, brother, you will be in love, really in love." Poor Alex. If only either of us could see the future. Luckily, we couldn't.

I was happy. Eva's visits to our winter quarters were always unexpected and always fun. She showed up in a chauffeur-driven ocean-green old Hudson, allocated to her by the state film company. She would whiz in and out, look at the books, look at the animals, and we would go for long walks in the winter woods. By now our relationship was intensely carnal. We knew every lean-to, hut, and sheltering hedge for miles. One of our favorite hideaways was a lean-to by the railway line. Its intended purpose was as a waiting room for the occasional traveler to Budapest. We once got so carried away in the wooden shack that we missed the train. We didn't even hear it. In company, I would look at her, aglow with pride and passion. I'd think, "This beautiful, cultured, tall blonde is mine—or at least she was a few hours ago."

We started filming again late next spring. According to script, our heroes are still lost in the mysterious world of the swamp. They meet a wild fisherman who navigates the reed jungle in a dugout canoe. It's a lucky encounter. He turns up just in time to save Chum, who is tangled up among the water lilies and is about to go down for the third and last time. The old man has trained his pet cormorant to catch fish for him. Fishing cormorants are a reality in China and Japan, not in Europe. Such details did not concern Comrade Director. He explained that we weren't doing cinema verite—"ours is a land of make-believe, magic, and enchantment. If it's entertaining, put it in the movie." He was probably right.

The dugout was an actual museum piece. The actor was too, in a way. The only man who was perfect for the part of the swamp rat was Gabor, our guide. Characters like Gabor should have become extinct about a century ago, but here he was. He had no acting experience; he didn't need it—he was actually playing himself. His whole appearance was faintly unbelievable. His face was creased and weathered as the lightning-scarred willows. His nose was the longest, sharpest, and most twisted I've ever seen on anyone. Naturally enough, we called him "Shrewnose." Never to his face, of course because we all loved him.

In the story, a villain, played by Alex, tries to steal the old man's cormorant. In one of the movie's main climaxes, he finally gets his hands on the coveted bird, only to be chased off by Chum. For this scene, we chose Outlaw, the strongest and most aggressive of our four Vizslas. He was a nice, friendly dog to everyone but Alex. For some reason, he had nothing but irrational hatred for Alex. I have seen this happen many times with animals, wild and domestic. Only the animal knows why; we can only guess. Conventional wisdom has it: "He must have been mean to him, or hit him, or . . ." That happens, certainly, but often there is no reason, at least not one that humans can understand. It's like that with us too. We talk to someone on the phone for five minutes. We don't know if he is good, bad, or ugly, honest or crooked, but when we hang up, the first thought is "I hate this son of a bitch." Bill Koehler, a trainer at Disney Studios, expressed it best when he was asked why some pit bulls bite. "Because they don't know how to use a handgun," said Bill.

On this occasion, Alex was the one who could have used a handgun. Comrade Director's viewpoint aside, this one scene in our movie was definitely cinema verite. Outlaw wanted a piece of Alex, and he got it. Alex was padded up as much as possible—layers of clothing and a motorcyclist's jacket and, under this, rags. For his hands, we devised a glove plated with pieces of flat bone. He would have been better off without it. The bone armor was not protection. Outlaw's fangs crunched right through, forcing a sliver of bone into his hand. Alex spent the next morning at the hospital having the bone removed and his wounds sewn up. Comrade Director congratulated both actors on a great performance. Outlaw didn't need it. He wasn't acting. He never bit Alex again, but from then on he was always cocky around him, as if to say "I did it to you once. I could do it again."

In the story, the villain escapes the dog by throwing a kerosene lamp. The burning lamp lands in some brush, sparking off the scene so beloved of animal movie-makers: the great forest fire. Our forest was a couple of acres of tinder dry reeds. For the dramatic end of the great fire, a huge herd of water buffalo stampedes through the blazing swamp, angry flames licking at their heels. Just one paragraph in the script but a different matter to shoot. We were surrounded by thousands of acres of reeds, but the way things worked out, we had to plant our own. Not an unusual irony in the movie world. They wouldn't let us start a fire within the reservation. So for back-breaking weeks we planted dry reeds in a two-acre open field.

The managers of the nearby state farm were happy to lend us their sixty-strong herd of buffalo. In the middle of our hand-planted reed jungle, we dug a pit. Into it, we sunk an eight-foot, presumably buffalo-proof, steel box for Comrade Director. From this vertical coffin, he could shoot up at the galloping tangle of black hooves.

With our preparations, complete, we found ourselves one morning looking at an immovable mass of cud-chewing bovines. They looked stubbornly back at us. These powerful, somber beasts are the closest relatives of the Cape buffalo, an animal that can chill the heart of any experienced African hunter. They are not the kind of animal that takes kindly to orders. To make them move at all would be an achievement, to make them run would be a miracle. But Adam had the answer, one that was obvious, safe, and humane.

We split the herd into two. The anchor group was corralled a hundred yards behind the camera dugout. The others, the action group, were enclosed in front of the camera. At the cry of "action!" the camera rolled, the gate was opened, and the action group ran to join their corralled friends, thundering over the dugout as they went. Despite how it looked on film, the flames came nowhere near their bovine heels. This was movie magic, created by burning a few bundles in a semi-circle in front of the camera.

When the scene was safely in the can, Comrade Director emerged from his earth. He was sweaty, sooty, muddy, and delighted. He patted my shoulder, "Well, my little fox-terrier, remember this years from now when we shoot our big Cape buffalo scene in Africa." He never set foot on African soil, but I did remember his words sixteen years later when I found myself in the middle of a charging Cape buffalo herd. But that's another story.

The big stampede scene was a gratifying end to our summer location shooting. In December of 1955, two cheetahs arrived at our winter quarters. They had been caught wild in Tanganyika and were to perform in our movie. Cheetahs in Hungary? Why not? The principle of "if it's entertainment, put it in the movie" always applied. The finale of *Pals* included a circus adventure in which the menace was provided by an escaped cheetah. The pair we got was a fully-grown male and female. I wanted to name them something exotic like Sinbad and Fatima, but Adam simply called the female "Lizzie" and the male "the Old One." These were the first wild cheetahs any of us had seen, much less worked with. All we had to go on were a few illustrations of maharajahs chasing antelope with trained cheetahs, or "hunting leopards," as they are sometimes called. But I read everything I could about them.

Adam's natural talent showed itself in its full potential. We had a large outdoor run and a smaller heated room for our valuable charges. From the very beginning, entering the cage was no problem. The male would charge, hissing and striking the floor with both front paws at the same time. We soon realized it was always a bluff. Most movie animals work through conditioned reflex. Out of soft willow wood, local craftsmen carved "calling spoons" for us. With these long handled spoons, we always fed the cats their daily portion of meat. Cheetahs rely on their eyesight more than any other sense, when hunting so they are very sensitive to visual clues. They soon learn to associate the sight of the spoon with food. The spoon becomes a sufficient stimulus to get them to move from point A to point B.

Training any animal is a step-by-step affair. With each step, you increase the animal's confidence. Most important, you never try to go too fast; you always adjust your progress to the individual animal's personality. Leash breaking came next. While eating, the cheetahs soon learned to like being scratched gently behind the ears and the side of the neck. Buckling on a strong leather collar was easy. Going for a walk met with a lot more resistance. Anyone who has tried to teach a house cat to walk on a leash has an idea of the problem we faced. Alex and I would snap two leashes to the collar. This allowed us to control the cat better, and also gave him a sense of security and guidance. Progress was slow: lurch to the right and flop, get up, take a few steps, lurch to the left, and flop again. Adam came up with an improvement: the waist band. This is a belt made of leather covered with silk, circling the cat's loins, and with a third leash attached. With the help of this third leash, one of us could sense when the cheetah was about to flop, and encourage him with a firm tug.

Our walks with these spotted half-cats became progressively longer and more enjoyable for all concerned. The maharajahs sometimes hooded their hunting cheetahs like a falcon. Darkness has a calming effect on animals and birds. We tried several designs for hoods, from round motor-cycle goggle contraptions to an enlarged falcon hood, but nothing would stay on. We never figured out how the Maharajahs did it. I am sure it's a very simple design but so is the wheel. Just try to make the first one.

When coming to a call, cheetahs start at a slow pace, shoulders hunched, eyes aimed at the trainer. They pick up speed as they come, ending with a lightning spurt over the last ten feet and a swipe at the spoon that is nothing but a blur. These arrow-swift rushes took us by surprise at first. On two occasions, we paid the hard way for our inexperience. I was calling the Old One from fifty feet, and, true to pattern, he stepped on the gas as he got closer. But this time, he overshot his goal, lashed out, and connected with my left hand. Unlike those of any other cat, a cheetah's four claws are dull and not retractable, but the dew-claw is as sharp as any leopard's. It tore open my left hand from the wrist to the fourth joint of the thumb. I had earned my first stripes for working with a big cat. Adam was philosophical: "It's a small price to pay for the experience of working with these magnificent animals. Besides, I'll probably be next." He was. Two weeks later, Lizzie swiped his face, leaving four gashes spread evenly from forehead to chin.

In time the cheetahs grew tamer and tamer. I had only one other scary moment with the Old One. He ripped a hole in a sensitive part of my pants and then, with surgical precision, extracted my handkerchief. Lizzie always remained skittish—quick to spit and hiss—but the Old One became tame enough to walk on a shoestring, anywhere.

In the fall of 1955, we were back on the Island of Cormorant. Comrade Director couldn't get enough of the simple yet hauntingly beautiful scenery. The domestic life of the cormorant always seemed to hold unlimited charms for him.

I shared a tent with Alex and the Old One. The weather was turning nippy, and it was important to keep the exotic cat warm. We burned wood in a small stove. Heat radiated into our tent while smoke escaped by a pipe that passed through an asbestos patch in the canvas wall. The Old One had his own cot, as comfortable as ours, except that his leash was tied securely to the frame. Late one afternoon, the crew was taking a well-earned tea break on Comrade Director's porch a few yards from the tent. There was no smoke and no warning. Suddenly, our tent was a mass of flame. Our immediate fear was for the life of the cheetah. We needn't have worried. Being tied to a bunk in a burning tent was a situation the Old One had no intention of tolerating. As soon as the flames started to roar, the frightened cat shot for the exit. His leash held fast, but the hardwood frame of the cot shattered as he put on a burst of record-breaking speed, living up to his reputation as the fastest mammal on earth. Once out of harm's way, the cat flopped, panting on the frosty grass as the tent became a pyramid of flame.

All my worldly belongings went up in smoke, including a new gray corduroy suit with which I hoped to impress Eva. Alex lost his dearest possession too: a recently acquired 16-guage shotgun. Ammunition exploded like fireworks as the tent collapsed.

The next day three strangers arrived. Their long leather coats told us who they were: investigators from state security and the film company. The Irish writer Brendan Behan once said he never saw a situation so dismal that the arrival of a policeman couldn't make it worse. And these were worse than ordinary policemen; they were from the AVH, or Allam Vedelmi Hatoshag: The Authority for the Defense of the State, the Hungarian KGB.

We, the crew, knew how the fire started. The radiating heat from the cast iron stove had ignited the dry canvas. A simple accident. But to the authorities, nothing is simple or accidental. The spooks poked around in the ashes, sniffing for sabotage. It was the makeup of the regime to suspect hostile acts in everything. The authorities were not concerned with our losses or feelings. Their concern was for the cheetah, which had cost the state hard currency. Could the American imperialists have had a hand in it? For days, the spooks probed and pried. They interrogated us separately, questioned us in groups, hinting that it would be better for the saboteur to fess up now, voluntarily. It would be much worse for us when the incriminating evidence, whatever that might be, turned up.

The fire itself was a horrifying experience. The interrogations that followed added a bitter taste of suspicion. This was just a small sample of what authority can do to people at its mercy. Eventually the spooks found other conspiracies to investigate and left us. Soon enough, the winter was over. In the spring of 1956, we unpacked the cameras for our third year of filming *Pals*. That season we shot in a new location—a resort in the Matra mountains two hundred miles to the northeast of Budapest.

By now, according to the script, Chum, Gossip, and Nimrod have made their way to the high country. These animals met more adventure and terrain than Rin Tin Tin, Silver, Lassie, and Flipper combined. The plot development seemed to be driven less by logic than by Comrade Director's insatiable appetite for changes in scenery. However, he remained firmly in charge of every detail. Working with him was demanding, but in general, fun. Take a typical instance: the day he decided that a scene needed the quiet tolling of a church bell in the background. Most directors leave such lowly takes to the sound man but not

Comrade Director. To get absolute quiet, we had to do the take at night. The communication between the sound recorder and the bell ringer broke down for some reason. During a state of minor confusion, Comrade Director's megaphoned voice boomed from the darkness. "I can see the situation has degenerated into f-cking around. I'm taking over." We got the take in one.

Adam and Alex stayed back at headquarters with the cheetahs, so I became the dog and bird trainer at the mountain location. Still not content with mountains and marshes alone, Comrade Director wrote an underground adventure for Chum. The dog somehow falls through a hole and wanders underground for days among the weird shapes of stalagmites and stalactites. How does he get out? Easy, an underground flash flood washes him to the surface.

There was plenty of water nearby in a raging mountain river. We needed a flood so Comrade Director decided to dam the river. Never mind that it was the driving force for the electrical turbines downstream and that damming it would cut off all power to a sizable city forty miles away. The only thing that matters to an obsessed director is his film. I have met several directorial monomaniacs since, but Comrade Director was one of a kind. First, he had a quiet talk with the engineer in charge of the generating plant—a man we called the Water King.

While the Water King watched, we built a giant wooden dam upstream of the generating plant. Soon the river slowed to a trickle, and the turbines stopped turning. Within an hour, the calls began coming in. The townspeople complained indignantly that their lights weren't working, and the river had dried up. The Water King, his pockets heavy with Comrade Director's money, growled back, "What do you want? Everyone knows that the river is capricious."

CHAPTER 5

SEVEN DAYS OF FREEDOM

I don't remember a milder, more pleasant autumn in Eastern Europe than that of 1956. One perfect day followed another like pearls on a necklace. In Hungary, we call these rare conditions "the old maid's summer." I don't know why—it's as logical as "Indian summer." All we knew or cared about then was that the warm days seemed endless. Nobody could guess that under the placid surface of everyday life, violent forces were gathering.

All films are shot out of sequence. After three years on *Pals*, we finally got around to filming the opening. After being jettisoned in crates from an airplane, the two dogs and hawk reach earth. Or water, in the case of Gossip. As the dachshund sinks toward a watery grave in the lake, Chum dives to the rescue. Adam joined us for this crucial sequence, and once again, I could admire his uncanny way with animals. To fetch objects from underwater is not easy for a dog. Some do it as play, but for the camera, play is not enough. When the director yells "Action," things must happen, and they should happen within a reasonable time. Comrade Director was a demanding but patient man. He always gave us ample time to prepare, but his advice was simple: "Son, if you want to stay in this business, you have two choices: get the action I want or you die."

Adam prepared Chum for the stunt. He used a combination of understanding, patience, many bits of sausage, and the occasional yank on the collar. Chum retrieved objects on land readily enough and from the shallows, but the shot called for something more ambitious. He was to dive seven feet under, then grab a crate by the handle and bring it to the surface. Gradually, Chum got used to deeper and deeper dives, but he soon ran into an inconvenient law of physics. His buoyancy prevented him from reaching the bottom. He'd get a yard under, then bob up like a cork. Even Adam was stumped. Tying weights to the dog was out of the question, and doing it in shallower water would lose the drama.

As so often happens in this business, it was the animals himself who came up with the solution. Chum discovered how to twist his muscular body and swim in such a way that he could corkscrew down to the bottom. This new technique took him easily to the muddy depths, where a dummy dachshund was gasping for air. For take after take, Chum dived, clamped his jaws around the handle of the crate, and dragged it to the surface. During this sequence I had my first ride in an airplane. As temporary special effects man, my job was to simulate engine trouble. Strapped to the fuselage, a thousand feet above the lake, I tossed bags of soot from the cargo door, while the jet stream tried to tear me loose. I loved every minute. Business class has never been that much fun.

On October 23, we heard news from Budapest that changed the course of my life. In a demonstration of solidarity with Polish workers, thousands of Hungarians marched on the radio building in Budapest. It was a peaceful demonstration. They sang as they marched and chanted patriotic slogans. But that most hated body of oppression, the AVH, opened fire. Hundreds of unarmed people died. This wasn't the first uprising in Eastern Europe, but it soon escalated to something unprecedented. Within hours, the unrest grew to become the most serious challenge to Russian rule from any captive nation. The news reaching us was contradictory and unreliable. The official government radio broadcast called the fighters "a small group of hooligans and enemy agents" and reassured us that "government forces supported by the brotherly troops of the Soviet Union are in total control." The day after the massacre, a crowd gathered at the radio station. They routed its "defenders," the AVH.

Filming was put on hold. Adam went to join his wife at the winter quarters. I was determined to go to Budapest by any means I could. I had a small 125 cc motorcycle, a cantankerous machine with the bad habit of letting me down when most needed. This time, it roared on for ten miles before the clutch burned out. I hitched a ride on a farmer's horse and buggy back to the movie set. There, I discovered that the crew's driver and head grip were just as adamant about getting to the center of the action as I was. We borrowed the company's Dodge 4-wheel drive and talked the local pump attendant out of a few gallons of rationed gasoline.

We set off for Budapest. We had to see for ourselves what was happening. And if there really was a resistance, we wanted to join it. A situation like this creates total uncertainty and an avalanche of rumors. We stopped hourly at larger settlements asking for information. Nobody knew anything definite, but the usual advice was "You made it so far, but at the next town there is a large Russian contingent or a troop of AVH. It will be impossible to get any further." We pushed on to the next town, and the next. Thirty-five miles from the capital we ran into a blockade. The road was torn up and barricades of timber and cobblestones made it impassable. For the first time, we could hear cannon fire and the screaming of Russian fighter planes.

We decided on an easterly detour. We could pass by our winter quarters and check how Adam and the rest of the crew were doing. About fifteen miles from our destination, we rounded a sharp bend and ran into a Russian tank. It smashed our left wheel, shredding the tire, and mangling part of the bumper. The Russians didn't even slow down. With its tracks squealing and grinding, the iron monster pushed us out of the way into the ditch. The soldier in the turret hurled out a torrent of guttural, Slavic curses at us—"Yobt faye Maty, Vengerski"—as his tank rumbled on its way.

With the help of a crowbar, a sledgehammer and determination, we straightened the bumper, put on the spare wheel and limped to base camp. Adam was overjoyed to see me. He had a plan, and he needed my help. We knew that in Budapest the freedom fighters were neutralizing the secret police. And our local representative of the AVH was still at his post. That night we knocked on his door and disarmed him. He seemed relieved. My first hostile act against the regime was a piece of cake.

The next morning, I went to Budapest. Even this close to the fighting, there was utter uncertainty. No one knew anything for sure. I started to walk. After a few miles, I reached a train station. An electric tram was about to leave in the right direction. There was something eerie about how normal it all looked. I climbed on, and in an hour I arrived in the eastern suburbs. Clara and Josef lived across the Danube on the western hills of Buda. I had no chance of making it by nightfall, and I could hear gunfire ahead of me. Luckily, I was near the zoo where Adam had an apartment. A neighbor gave me the key, and I spent the night there. I turned on the radio and heard the announcer identify the station as the Free Radio of Hungary. We had a new government, a new prime minister and minister of defense. Negotiations were underway with the Soviets for a complete withdrawal of all their forces.

An incredible warm feeling came over me. Only someone who has experienced a true miracle, something unexpectedly wonderful, a miraculous cure of a relative, or even more profound, the resurrection of a loved one, a feeling of such joy that comes only once in a lifetime—for a few people. After more than a decade of foreign domination, we were free. Freedom becomes really precious only when we lose it. Until then, it's taken for granted, like breathing. For eleven years, I felt that even my breathing was controlled by the state and by the searching eyes of big brother. Oh yes, we had good times too, but the heavy arm of oppression was never too far from our consciousness.

I recalled a field trip in a western border town where from the lookout tower we could see Austria. The free Western world. The longing that came over me to be a member, a citizen, of that society, was almost painful. And now these incredible words from the wireless as I sat in the darkness: "This is the free radio of Hungary." Slow, warm tears of joy came to my eyes, and I felt the world opening up for my small, long suffering homeland.

The next morning, I left the apartment and went out into the street. I wanted to find out if Clara and Josef were all right. There was no phone and, of course, no public transport. I could only walk. The inner city was a wasteland. All around me were scenes that only a Goya or a Doré could capture. At street corners were the blackened hulks of tanks and trucks, locked together like the creations of a demented sculptor. Buildings that once were beautiful had been reduced to rubble. The Kilian Barracks was still standing, but its corner had been sliced away from to top to bottom, like the victim of a mad giant with a bread-knife. Here and there lay the bodies of patriots, huddled under the red, white and green of the Hungarian flag. But most horrible of all were the Russian dead. They were left where they fell. The citizens afforded them no dignity. Their only shroud was a coating of lime to hasten decomposition. They lay there, grotesque, as if they alone had been singled out for death by an early winter storm.

Szena Square was a bizarre mess. It was carpeted entirely with bales of colored silks dragged from a broken storefront. The silk was soaked with gallons and gallons of oil. Two blackened tanks gave me a clue as to what happened. Some untrained military geniuses—kids, as it turned out—had improvised a tank trap. When the Russian tanks entered the square, their treads spun hopelessly on the slippery silk and oil. They became sitting ducks for the young military geniuses and their Molotov cocktails.

Another school-age kid turned his mother's thick, homemade jam into a weapon. He ran in under a tank's arc of fire and smeared plum jam on the driver's window. This slowed the tank down for a few seconds. A few seconds are all you need to demolish a tank with a petrol bomb. Most of our stories were like that. Full of courage and humor. And we Hungarians were not the only heroes of these stories. I heard about a group of elderly British nannies that kept a stiff upper lip throughout the upheaval. Nannies from Kensington were much in demand in the old days by upper crust Hungarians who liked the idea of their children being raised in the British nursery tradition. Some of these gentle ladies fell in love with Hungary and stayed. During the worst of the fighting, a Miss Westbrook called the British Consulate in a state of alarm. The consul told her to keep calm and offered to get her safely back to England. But her problem was bigger than that. "Oh no, my dear," she chirped. "I wouldn't let the Russians ruin my life. But I am in a terrible fix. I have just run out of Brooke Bond tea."

Hungarians tend to have that kind of sangfroid too, which may explain why we liked the nannies so much. Unlike the British, however, we have made a tradition out of revolution. We have at least one a century. The last one had happened in 1848. Now I was witnessing another uprising—a fiercely patriotic nation saying, "We've had enough."

Dazed as I was, I took pictures on my walk to Buda. From many rooftops waved the flag of the revolution. It was like the old Hungarian flag, except that it had a proud, gaping hole where the offensive red star had been removed. That star was the symbol of oppression. At one point, a piece of sandstone smashed on the pavement in front of me. A sculpted star, pried loose from the façade of a public building. I heard an old man remark: "The stud star is coming down at last. That's what has been f-cking us for the past eleven years." For days people were climbing public buildings and prying the hated stars loose. All over the city, they fell like meteors on an August night.

One of the miracles of the Hungarian revolution was that there was no looting. Goods remained untouched behind broken store windows. At many street corners, open suitcases lay, full of money. Nobody touched it. Passersby would add cash and banknotes to overflowing cases. People were dying all over the city. These collections were to help the newly orphaned children. There was no looting—with one exception. I saw people take roses, carnations, and chrysanthemums from a shattered flower shop. They placed them on the red, green, and white flags that covered the fallen heroes. At an intersection lay a bronze statue of Stalin, like a gigantic dead cockroach. A throng of men and women seemed to be feasting on the body, hammering fragments off it to keep as triumphant souvenirs. Josef Visarionovich Dsugasvili, who named himself Stalin because it meant "man of steel," had not surrendered his granite perch easily. Even powerful trucks and thick ropes couldn't budge him. It took a pair of cutting torches to sever him at the knees and bring him toppling to the pavement. Only his jack-boots remained on the pedestal—one of them acting as a makeshift vase for the new Hungarian flag. Folk humor instantly renamed Stalin Square: Boot Square.

In the spring of 1956, three years after Stalin's death, Kruschev denounced him at a secret party congress. The Soviet premier's belated courage was a gift to the Budapest joke-smiths. They swore on the best authority that Stalin's statue was going to be replaced by a giant, bronze pigeon. At least the pigeons had the guts to shit on him before he died.

As I walked, the profusion of images—horrible, bizarre, and humorous—was baffling. Only my feelings were clear. From the faces around me, I knew that others felt it too. Our beautiful Budapest was battered but still proud. Crossing the chain bridge, I saw that the Danube was more beautiful than ever. The bridge is guarded by four majestic stone lions: two at either end. They are tongue-less, and legend has it that the sculptor leaped to his death from the bridge when he realized his omission. It seemed to me then that Hungary had been voiceless too long. We had found our tongues at last. We could speak freely without fear of communist stool pigeons. The battle was over. We had won our freedom and were full of hope.

I found Josef and Clara in euphoria. We drank tea and we talked. Can we really have won? There were still some big questions to be answered. Will the Russians leave us alone now? Can they afford to take a beating from a small nation—or to be more exact, a handful of students, a few thousand workers, and a few units of the Hungarian army? According to Russian propaganda, foreign mercenaries had fought on our side. But we knew the truth. Ironically, the only foreign help we had was Russian: deserters who saw the justice in our cause. We were free, but the biggest question still hung in the air. Will we stay free? We didn't need to wait long for the answer. We had seven days, seven days of freedom, before the iron fist struck again.

I stayed with Josef and Clara throughout the week. On the night of November 3rd, the whole city was lit by thousands of flickering lights. It was All Saints Day, when traditionally we lit candles on the graves of loved ones. This time, people put candles in their windows. It was like some kind of mass premonition. We were lighting candles not for the dead, but for those about to die. The invasion of the Suez Canal by British and Israeli forces that November couldn't have come at a worse time for us. The world's attention was diverted. The Russians seized the occasion to smash the resistance. They brought thousands of fresh troops, many of them Mongolians from Asia. In the hours before dawn on November

4th, without warning or provocation, they pounced. Like hellish fireworks, incendiary shells rained on the sleeping city.

Tanks rumbled down the main avenues, firing at random into houses. Buildings crumbled into clouds of dust. Buildings fell, but the real target was the morale of the Hungarian people. I slipped out of the house before dawn. I stuck to the backstreets as I went in search of a former school friend. I could hear cannon shells exploding and the crackle of rifle-fire. Tanks were grinding through the main streets. They didn't worry me. Far more deadly was what you didn't hear: stationary tanks and armored personnel carriers. They waited at intersections and picked off their victims with machine guns.

I made my way carefully through the city. Five miles away, my school friend, Imre, was living with his Uncle Victor. Imre studied civil engineering, but he'd also acquired military knowledge at an army-run summer camp. Imre felt as bitterly towards the Soviet invaders as I did. Better still, in his unsuspecting uncle's loft, he had hidden two machine pistols. When I arrived, Imre was ready to go. The machine pistols were Russian made. The drum-shaped magazine made them look like something Al Capone would use. They were simple, even crude, in their construction and turned out to be brutally effective. Imre's sarcastic nickname for the weapon was "the Russian guitar."

In the corridor outside the apartment, Imre gave me a quick lesson in guerrilla warfare. His instructions were short and to the point. You slap the magazine in with two quick movements. To switch to fully automatic, slide the catch forward; back again for single firing. It was easy to remember, he explained. "Think of it this way. Push forward for all the bullets you want to give to the enemy. Pull it toward you for the one you will need for yourself." In the next three days, I completed my education. From the very beginning, we, and the thousands like us who took to the streets, knew the cause was lost. We fought in anger and bitterness because we had to. We fought for ourselves and our pride as Hungarians.

Imre and I darted from building to building, firing our machine pistols from broken windows, from behind piles of rubble. When we ran out of ammunition, someone always knew where to find more. Imre's practical skills were as good as his theories. He told me to "Never, ever stay long in one place. And never check the results of your firing." That advice surely saved my life. A split second of curiosity cost the lives of many young women and men in these street battles. You must fire a short burst and change location as fast as your feet can carry you. Never look back. The Russian reply was often only a split second in coming. If you stayed a moment too long, the whole building would collapse around you, blown to bits by cannon fire from Russian tanks. That is the effective way to discourage resistance.

And inevitably we were discouraged. Imre and I dodged and fired for three days. When exhausted or hungry, we would hide our guns somewhere and go home for a meal and rest. We tried to keep up our spirits, but hope leaked away. No city, no matter how courageous and determined its inhabitants, can resist such overwhelming forces. The military might that the Soviet Union unleashed on Hungary was equal to the combined forces of Rommel and Montgomery at the battle of El Alamein. I fired hundreds of rounds with my Russian guitar. It never jammed. The last magazine I fired will live in my memory forever. I was sprinting between two buildings, dangerously exposed, out in the open with the gun twitchy and ready, set at fully automatic. I almost made it across when a Russian truck tore around the corner. Standing on the running board was a soldier with a machine pistol. It was exactly the same model as mine. We saw each other at the same time.

In a half arc, I cover the vehicle, driver, and rider. The machine pistol in my hand stops bucking. I am out of ammo. In slow motion the truck veers away. It ploughs into a lamp post, and the driver's head breaks the windshield. The torso of the soldier buckles forward, then hits the pavement. I dropped the gun down a coal chute in the next building. Imre and I had had enough of the fighting.

During the days of victory, I had bluffed a motorcycle out of the state film company. We climbed on it and at once hit the road. We would go to the countryside to see how our folks had survived the revolution of 1956. The only serious resistance by now was from an island in the Danube. This was the largest industrial center in the country, the pride and joy of the communist regime, the so-called "red island of Csepel." So much for communist solidarity—the workers on this island were still fighting. The shiny new motorcycle carried us up the hill beyond Budapest. Near the top we stopped and looked down on the city, as if from the balcony of a giant theater. Inching towards Csepel, like a black snake, was a Russian convoy of trucks and tanks. A group of Hungarian freedom fighters approached us. They wanted to know if we knew anything about artillery.

I was not surprised to hear Imre say that he did. We climbed a cliff to where an old, dull green anti-aircraft gun sulked in a vineyard. There were a few boxes of ammunition too. The gun had evidently been abandoned. We guessed that from the helmets scattered around it. It was designed to shoot planes out of the sky, but the Russian convoy in the valley seemed too good a target to pass up. Imre quickly figured out how to load the towering weapon. Aiming was another matter entirely. My friend had plenty of ideas, although he was by no means an artillery officer. Somehow, we managed to crank the gun in the general direction of the convoy.

Our first greeting missed by a mile. The convoy didn't bother to stop. The next shell burst closer, and the fourth and fifth managed to shower hot iron on the long black serpent. That did it. The Russians returned our fire with their own artillery. Shells exploded a few hundred feet from us. The helmets lying around us, so far unused, found owners in seconds. We fired the rest of the ammunition and slipped away among the grapevines.

That night, we shared an empty farmhouse with the enterprising guerillas. The next morning, we left our hosts and headed for a college town nestled in the peaceful hills of Trans-Danubia. We had hoped to stay with one of Imre's cousins. When we arrived, his teachers told us we were too late. The cousin had left for the Austrian border the previous day. After we reassured him that we had no guns, the parish priest gave us a bed. We spent the night in serious discussion. Life in Hungary was likely to be even more oppressive now.

Reprisals were inevitable. I had been planning my defection for years, since the beginning of the occupation. I was going to make the break as soon as *Pals* was finished. But all the signs seemed to indicate that now was the time to go. The country was in chaos. Just last summer, unexpectedly, the minefields that snaked along the Austrian border had been removed. And the invading Russian army had stopped a few miles from the border. It wouldn't have been smart for them to pose for the telephoto lenses of Western reporters. I had made up my mind. An opportunity like this comes once in a hundred years.

Imre didn't want to leave. Not yet. He had two years of studies left, and as a man with a diploma he would have a better chance in the West. But he would come with me as far as the frontier. The next morning we left the good priest and headed for the border and my appointment with the future. We were not the only travelers on that road. After our brutal defeat, a sense of hopelessness descended like a tangible shroud. Eleven years under the communist heel was long enough. Two hundred thousand Hungarians used the only vote they had: their feet. Until the middle of December, it was relatively easy to leave. People went by train, by horse-drawn wagon, by trucks, by tractors, some pushing their meager belongings in a wheelbarrow. Imre and I rode the motorcycle. It was so new it didn't have a license plate. Ten miles along the road, a Russian tank stopped us. I had studied the language of Lenin for four years at school, but I hated it so much I learned almost nothing. I stammered two of the dozen or so Russian words I remembered. I said, "Mu idyom." The young tank commander seemed to appreciate my command of his language. "Mu idyom" means "We are going."

Later on, in no-man's-land, we were challenged by a patrol of Hungarian border guards. "Where are you going, boys?" This time I didn't have to contend with the language barrier. "To Vienna. Do you mind?" I said. The guard gave a friendly wave. "Go ahead. We'll probably join you later." At the border, Imre told me to take the bike. He would find his way back to his parents somehow. We said an emotional farewell. For a souvenir, he took a red and white Austrian flag. I watched for a long time as he walked deeper and deeper into the gray November evening. I turned towards Austria. I was leaving behind the sad, defeated land of a brave little nation. I was thinking, "Will I ever see my best friend again?"

CHAPTER 6

WELCOME TO VIENNA

few minutes later, I reported at an Austrian gendarme post. I had vague buccaneer notions of keeping the motorbike—the spoils of war after all—but although I had arrived in the West, it wasn't the Wild West. The only piece of paper I had on the machine said, "Owner: Documentary and Newsreel Film Company, Budapest." My shiny burgundy red steed, which I had ridden to freedom, was locked in an Austrian warehouse. Months later, the film company reclaimed it. That night, along with thousands of other refugees, I took a train ride to Treuskirchen, a major refugee camp just outside Vienna.

Many years later, I still take my hat off in deep gratitude to the people and leaders of Austria. They opened their arms to this unexpected Eastern invasion, to this loud, ill-fed, shabbily clothed, sometimes bad-mannered sea of displaced persons deposited by a brief storm of history on their doorsteps. I spent one night in camp, and wouldn't you know it, I had the first serious attack of homesickness. It was prompted by a strange catalyst: a trash bucket exactly like the one we used for picking up after the cheetahs. By strange association, I started to think of

Adam, the Old One, Lizzie, Alex, and the rest of the crew I'd just left behind. It was a serious attack, but I had little time to indulge it.

I did know someone in Austria. During the bucolic pre-war days, Rita, an Austrian lass, came to visit us practically every summer. She was a friend of my mom and Aunt Clara and forever in love with my uncle, Paul the Handsome. I gave her address almost as an afterthought to the Austrian official. Shortly after that, the camp loudspeaker wanted me. I had a visitor. We hadn't seen each other in fourteen years, but Rita hugged me like a long lost relative. She was now married and had a teenage son. She rescued me from the camp and took me to her nice apartment in a fashionable part of Vienna.

Machine gun fire woke me from a deep sleep. Groggily, I dove for my weapon under the bed, sure that I was back in war-torn Budapest. Of course, I couldn't find my Russian guitar. The gunfire turned out to be the staccato noise of a jackhammer tearing up the pavement. I was in a friendly but strange land, gathering first impressions. My high-school German came back in leaps and bounds. To me, the charming Austrian city was like a distant planet. Shops full of exotic goods. Dazzling lights. The rush-hour traffic on Mariahilfe Strasse, creeping like a mechanized glacier. I saw my first electric gasoline pump. Back in Hungary, all we had was the hand-cranked, dual-cylinder type. Filling my motorbike used to take considerable muscle and time—these marvels satiated the tank of a Mercedes in seconds.

Rita bought me a new wardrobe to replace my leather motorcycle outfit and heavy boots. In the shoe store, the salesman stuck my foot under a tube. I could watch the bones of my toes fitting snug in the shoe. What marvels of technology. Rita was my guardian angel. Her husband was a curmudgeon. It was obvious their marriage was not a good one, and my presence made it no better. I started to hunt for a job. I went to the zoo, talked to circus directors, and told them about my expertise with dogs, birds, and of course the wonderful cheetahs. They clucked politely. That was all. The mail wasn't exactly overflowing with offers. What I really needed was a few of my pictures—visible evidence of my prowess as an animal trainer.

On a foggy evening in late December, I had just returned from a visit to the museum of natural history. Rita greeted me in the hallway with a mysterious

smile. "I have a surprise for you." Sprawled in an easy chair, grinning from ear to ear, was my guerrilla warfare instructor, my wandering friend, Imre. This is the man I wasn't going to see for years, or perhaps forever. "I changed my mind," he said matter-of-factly. "Two years is a long time to wait for a Communist diploma. I think I can get a scholarship here and finish my studies." For weeks, we explored Vienna. The future was hanging around the periphery of my consciousness, but why hurry?

Imre did get a Rockefeller scholarship and settled in a student home. It was slowly dawning on me that Austria might not be the country for my very specific qualifications. My horizons started to expand. I made inquiries internationally, but I still felt I needed pictures—more proof of what I do, what I can do. In January I met two refugees at the student home. Bela and John were leaving to study in Canada. Bela was booked to fly the next day, and John was going to follow him later. He wanted to visit his folks in Hungary one last time. The fact that the border was now closed and closely guarded didn't worry him. He was an expert in crisscrossing the frontier, having evaded the patrols countless times. He was planning one last infiltration.

Before I knew what I was saying, it was out. "John, let me go with you." He looked at me, astonished. What I had to say did sound crazy: "You see your parents; I make my way back to Budapest, pick up my negatives to help with my job hunting, and in a week we'll be back in Vienna, drinking a toast in the Mathiaskeller." I tried to make it sound reasonable, but this was certainly the dumbest move I ever made in my life. I wouldn't take a risk like that now if someone offered me the coronation jewels of the Tsar. John explained that it wasn't quite as simple as that. The border wasn't a sieve any more. There were patrols, guard towers, dogs. The whole frontier zone, a twenty-four-mile strip bordering Austria, was heavily controlled. If you didn't have an internal passport stating that you lived in this forbidden strip, your chances were slim to none. They'd pick you up before you got halfway to Sopron. And then... It didn't bear thinking about. And if you think it can't happen to you . . .

As a native of Sopron, John had his internal passport. But his friend, the Canada-bound student, had one too. He handed a thin, dark-red booklet to me. "I don't think I'll need this in Alberta. You can have it, pretty stamps and all."

The pages of the passport were covered in the rubber-stamped symptoms of that incurable disease: bureaucracy.

And so, on a cold night in 1957, John and I slipped back into Hungary. Having two passports didn't do anything for my nerves. If they caught me, I would be in serious trouble. Since then, I have analyzed my motives for this reckless move a hundred times. Did I really do it to get my photos? Partly. Or was it for the sheer spine-tingling excitement of it all? Also partly. I had defected on the spur of the moment. And deep down, though I hardly admitted it then, even to my own searching soul, was the constant companion of all fresh immigrants: homesickness. I was haunted by the faces of my relatives: especially by the sad eyes of my grandmother whom I adored. I wanted to see them all once more, if only to say goodbye. I wanted to see once more what I was leaving behind. Is freedom, a chance to travel, so important? Is money? Are these lures strong enough to leave the land where I was born, the language I knew? I thought of Comrade Director on a good day calling me "you little fox terrier," and Eva's special smiles in my direction. Going back was insane. But I had to go. We crossed no-man's land at two in the morning. We trudged across ploughed fields in the dark for a mile or two, and began to breathe easier, when we ran into a border patrol.

Actually, we didn't run; they just stepped out of a bush like shadows wearing machine guns.

"Where to, boys?"

"To town," we stammered.

"Where from?"

"Vienna."

And then, "What the hell do you think the border is, a revolving door?"

We ended up at the headquarters of the border police. We were not alone. A number of returnees waited in a large, cold, inhospitable room. My homesickness started to evaporate like summer rain on the hot pavement. Luckily, they didn't search me, so nobody found my conflicting documents. I stuck the false one in a crack under the long table. John and I got our stories straight: "We changed our minds; the West is not for us. We are coming back to our poor parents once and for all." I spent the rest of the night trying to sleep on the table.

In the morning, they began leading the detainees one by one into the shining presence of Lieutenant Marko. Cold and hungry as we were, the name of our interrogator chilled us more— the toughest jail in the country is located on Marko Street in Budapest. My turn came at two in the afternoon. This wasn't my first interrogation. In high school, somebody punched out the eyes of a Stalin poster, and naturally, as a member of Class X, the finger of suspicion pointed at me. And after the tent fire, Alex and I were grilled by state security. Those incidents were unnerving enough, but compared with my present situation, they were mere confessionals.

Marko was short and powerful. His face was pocked, and he had the small, suspicious eyes of a wild boar.

"Why did you defect?"

"I work for the movies. I wanted to see some Western films.

"In other words, you are an adventurer."

The way he said "adventurer," it sounded like a combination of mass murderer and traitor.

"No, not really," I answered feebly. "I am a falconer."

"You mean like a count or baron of the old exploiting classes?" He had an answer for everything. "You ride around with a bird on your hand."

"Not like that at all. I had, er, have a job with the state film company. I train them, and Comrade Director films them."

"Whom did you meet in the West?"

"Quite a few people."

"You know who I mean," he thundered. "People who could interest us. The enemies of socialism."

Marko looked like the average wild boar but may not have been as smart. He set a trap for me with a clumsiness that was almost comical: "When did you say you met the agents of the FBI and CIA?"

Scared as I was, I felt a more terrifying urge to giggle. The merest hint of a smile could have been disastrous.

"I said when did you meet the agents of—"

"I didn't."

My answer didn't please him.

"Who was the interpreter at the refugee camp?" he asked.

I thought it best to hand him a small victory. I began to talk. I created a flashy redhead wearing green riding britches, speaking German, French, English, and possibly Sanskrit. My inquisitor wrote down the details. The tip of his tongue followed the slow path of his pencil. He liked my story. For the rest, I stuck to what John and I had agreed.

"I left temporarily, and now, I am back for good. I couldn't leave my poor widowed mother alone."

Finally, after a stern warning, he let me go. "I hope we don't meet again. Because if we do . . ." His voice trailed off. I saw a vision of a cat of nine tails, my fingers gripped in a vice, and comrade Marko approaching with a pair of hoof cutters.

They escorted me back to the big room. I found my borrowed passport still wedged under the table. By six in the evening, we were turned loose. We headed straight for John's former landlady's garden where he dug up a glass jar filled with money. He called it his Austro-Hungarian bank. Now that we had funds, we made plans. Come hell or high water, we would meet at John's home in four days. We shook hands and boarded our trains.

In a few hours I was back in Budapest. As I was walking up the slope to our house, I saw my mother walking towards me. She looked at me blankly and walked right past me. I called after her, "Mother, don't you recognize me, your only son?" She pivoted as if a charge of electricity hit her. "Is it really you? It can't be. My son is in Vienna. I finally got a postcard from him last week." The rest of my folks were just as incredulous, but at least they recognized me. I went to see Adam, and he gave me one last piece of advice: "You'll make it back again, and when you do, remember: your heart, your only talent, lies with animals. As you learn the language of your new homeland, get a job in this field. Don't you dare to be a chauffeur, or elevator boy, or even a photographer. Stay where your love and talent lies—with animals and birds." He also gave me a present. An eight-month-old Vizsla. She was Chum's daughter, and her name was Chardash, the national dance of Hungary. Defecting was going to be hard enough without the added burden of a pup, but I didn't even think about that. She was irresistible, as all Vizsla puppies are.

In Budapest, I collected some pictures and negatives, the main reason for my foolish journey, and boarded a train to meet John. I had covered one leg of a 400-mile triangle. Point A, our entry point and capture, was 150 miles away. I was at Point B, Budapest, and now I had to get to John's hometown, Point C, before crossing to Point A again. Point A was a short hop to freedom, but it was also where the specter of Lieutenant Marko loomed.

After the evening meal at John's house, we cleared the table and I started to work on my masterpiece. I had to doctor my false document, the one given to me by Bela, who was, by now, safely in Canada. I had to do it very carefully, as if my life depended on it, and it probably did. Bela and I were roughly the same age. I couldn't say that for our height—I am six feet tall, and the original owner of the passport was five-foot-four. Oh well, I had to leave something to luck. I did an excellent job swapping photos. With a Gillette blade, I peeled out his and glued in mine. The concave dry stamp running through the corner of the picture created a bit of a problem. I used calipers, two nails, and a miniature screwdriver for this important forgery. When the job was done, John and his family agreed that Sherlock Holmes himself would not suspect a thing.

We took the train again to complete the last leg of the triangle to Point A— hopefully skipping Lieutenant Marko's hospitality. Long before the hero of the movie *Midnight Express* took his frightening ride on the Istanbul train, I spent five heart-choking hours on the shuttle to freedom. As we were getting closer to the border, the inspections became more frequent. Pairs of guards, wearing the green epaulettes of border police, checked my forged passport fourteen times. I tried to make myself small and insignificant, trying to shrink to five-foot-four. If the inspection took longer than the eternity of ten seconds, I would start petting Chardash. By bending down, I hoped to look even smaller. The puppy returned my gaze as if she had known me all of her life—all eight months of it. It was clear to the most hairy-hearted ogre of a guard that a team like us couldn't possibly contemplate defection to the imperialists. The train slid into Sopron at nine in the evening. At the exit, a final check. Two guards fingering machine guns stand on either side of the narrow gate. Behind them, looming through the semi-darkness, a paddy wagon waited, its open doors ready to swallow any suspicious persons.

A short bark of a command: "Identifications." With stooping shoulders, and keeping my eyes lowered, I hand my papers over. Chardash licks the man's greasy boot. My paper is handed back. John is behind me. The fools! They let us go. The next morning at four o'clock, we walked into Austria. Nothing could stop us now. Chardash followed on her leash as silently as a ghost. The frontier, at this point, was marked by a narrow ditch. As I jumped it, the puppy's leash broke. She hesitated on the muddy divide between East and West. I whispered, "Chardash, come here." In a second she was at my side, wagging her tail, as if saying, "Of course, I'm coming. Do you think I want to grow up a Russian puppet?"

Rita and Imre were overjoyed at my second defection, and we did have our celebration, as planned, at the Mathiaskeller. Chardash was a big hit. She even conquered Rita's usually morose husband, and Rita agreed to keep her temporarily. This temporary room and board turned out to last nearly two years. Time didn't stand still. I had to make plans to find a country to settle in. Adam had a friend in West Germany: Zoltan von B. He was a wildlife expert and game breeder with connections reaching as far as East Africa. I wrote a long letter to him explaining who I was, what I did. I also included some photos of my birds and animals in action. At the same time, I applied for a West German visa, German being the only language I spoke besides my mother tongue.

I soon received a reply from Zoltan. He was very polite and extremely understanding and essentially told me to learn another trade. My aristocratic hobbies would get me nowhere except the poorhouse. It was déjà vu, like listening to my Uncle Josef the Strict. Basically, I wasn't really surprised, but I also had no intention of learning another trade.

I met a reporter from *Life* magazine. She said, "Why don't you go to America? A profession like yours needs a large, rich country, where there is room for people with off-beat occupations." So far it had never occurred to me to emigrate to the United States. My number one handicap being the total lack of English. I'd studied Latin, German, and four years of Russian were forced upon us, but not a drop of the language of Shakespeare. America seemed immensely far away. Its customs, or what I knew of them, were totally different and worrisome. But what the hell, I applied for a visa anyway. In ten days I received permission to enter the

United States as a resident alien. It was a good feeling, laced with apprehension. I would have rather stayed in Europe, but I had to make my move.

On my last evening at Rita's, I was listening to Radio Free Europe. Refugees were sending coded messages to relatives left behind. One of them said, "Alex sends many greetings to his parents in the street of peacocks. He is well, and he is leaving for America soon." I was overjoyed. That could only be my Alex, the perpetually lovesick Alex. Until then, I had no idea what happened to him. And now, like me, he was on his way to America. Most of the refugees were already dispersed to the four corners of the globe. Australia, Canada, and America were the most popular places, but I doubt if there is a one-horse town anywhere on this planet where you won't find the odd Hungarian.

I shared touching goodbyes again from Rita, whose kindness I could never repay, and my best friend, Imre. God knows where he got hold of it, but as we parted he presented me with a five-dollar bill. A small cardboard suitcase easily held all my belongings. I didn't need much. I was twenty-one, after all, and physically and mentally ready for the big jump. At the airport, we were standing in line ready to board when I got a call from Rita. "Your West German visa has arrived." I thought about it for ten seconds. I told her, "I am going to America." I could hear her voice trembling, and mine wasn't too steady either. I could only thank her. Then I joined the long line of refugees in the belly of the big silver bird.

CHAPTER 7

"GIVE ME YOUR POOR, DOWNTRODDEN, AND CONFUSED"

1957–1964

t was before the age of jets. I'm not sure how many hours it took to reach the East Coast, but it was a long time. First stop: Shannon, Ireland. Our next landing was in Reykjavik. I used part of my five-dollar fortune to send postcards of Icelandic geysers, telling the folks back home "I made it halfway." Our next stop was unscheduled. The outside starboard motor began to cough and sputter and stopped. The rest of the propellers continued to churn the thin air, but there was something disquieting about the one motionless propeller just outside my window and the icebergs waiting below. A young lady next to me turned pale and asked why I was so relaxed. I told her that I trusted the pilot was just as concerned about reaching land as we were. "Besides, a machine like this could make it on one motor, if the worst comes to the worst." She seemed relieved at this reassurance from a seasoned flier. "You've obviously flown before," she said. "That must make a difference." I wanted to enhance my image as a man of the world by telling her that on my only previous flight I was chucking bags of soot out to simulate engine failure for the movie cameras, but I thought better of it.

An hour later, we made a smooth emergency landing at Sarassuak air base in Greenland. The weather was bone chilling, but the mess-hall was toasty with the smell of standard Air Force cooking. To me, the eggs and pancakes were as welcome as a banquet at the Ritz. I overheard a young refugee mother telling her son, "Here, my son, you can drink all the Coca-Cola you want." She made it sound like a duty, a badge of American patriotism. As if drinking Coke, lots of it, was life's most desirable achievement.

The next morning, our bird was mended and we took off. One more stop—at Gander, in Newfoundland—and on March 13, 1957, we touched down on American soil. It was the middle of the night. Buses took us to Camp Kilmer in New Jersey. The first impressions flashing by in the dark night are still in front of me. Semi-trailers, looming like railroad cars on the pavement. A neon sign of a boy holding a bun, and a neon dog wagging his tail. I had no idea what they were advertising, but I knew I liked it.

At the camp itself, there were so many Hungarians it was like arriving in a medium sized town in the old country. The next morning, I met George, our special effects man from *Pals*. He already had a lucrative business going. He painted idealized portraits of our soldier guides and their relatives. Members of the US army, many of them second-generation immigrants, were our helpers, nurses, and interpreters.

Adam's older brother, Nick, and his wife, Maria, lived in New York City. Nick defected years ago and spoke perfect English, German, French, and Italian. They were also two of the most unselfish people I met, bar none. I went to see them in New York. I surfaced at the Port Authority bus terminal, marveled at the endless rows of movies in Times Square, and craned my neck to see the tops of the skyscrapers. Nick and Maria assured me that they would help me in any way they could. They would have done it anyway, but Adam's letter, in which he mentioned that I was the closest thing to a son he ever had, certainly helped.

Life in Camp Kilmer wasn't bad at all. There was lots of good food, movies, and television. The kids wanted to see nothing but cowboys, cowboys, and more cowboys. There were courses in English, and we were interviewed about our wishes for employment. I could have spent a couple of months at Camp Kilmer easily, but that's not the effective American way. In ten days, I had a job. Destination: Miami, Florida.

It wasn't quite clear to me what kind of place hired me, but it had something to do with birds. If it's birds, it's okay. And the owner was of German descent, which helped with the language problem. A few days later, in the hot, smoggy airport of Miami, a confused young immigrant sweated in a stiff, artificial leather jacket, looking around, waiting for something to happen. I saw my name on a cardboard and started to talk to the man in German, but he just shook his head. The owner couldn't make it. It was the son and his beautiful wife who came to meet me. In my confusion, I kissed her hand like in a movie. I might have even clicked my heels like a Prussian Officer. If I was to be strange and foreign, I may as well be stranger and foreigner. They dropped me off with a retired couple who sub-rented a room to me. In the humid Florida night, I fell into an exhausted sleep. The next morning, the owner showed me around, how to shop at a supermarket, buy a meal at an automat, use a coin laundry—all the little things taken for granted by everyone except a Martian and me.

My place of work was Parrot Paradise. It was a beautifully landscaped, manicured tourist attraction featuring tropical birds, mostly of the parrot family. There was a trained bird show that gave me my first and probably only inferiority complex as a trainer. Those noisy hook-billed parrots and cockatoos did an endless number of amazing tricks. Not that I had to worry right away about proving myself as a trainer. The birds had a larger vocabulary than I. Until I picked up some English I was given a broom with a nail in the handle and a scoop, and every morning I would pick up bits of paper, cigarette butts, empty Coke cans—in a word, rubbish—in the parking lot. Intellectually, not the most satisfying position, but I realized, without English, how would I talk to the birds?

I started to learn. I had two schoolbooks and a dictionary, read headlines and comic strips, and for a month took evening courses. Two young men at the park—Walter, a freckle-faced Scot, and Parnell, a black—befriended me, and in a short while we were having conversations of a sort.

English is one of the few languages easier to speak than to understand. I could make myself understood before my ear adjusted to the alien sounds. And when I got to understand a bit, I got confused again. Florida was in the Deep South, y'all hear? There was a charming lady, Mrs. Moon, in charge of baby birds. She tried to teach me Canadian: "aout and abaot." Bill, the bird dietician, came from Brooklyn. Why on earth did he say "goil" instead of girl, and who on earth should I listen to as my pronunciation guide? Walter the Scot rolled his Rs worse than an Italian, and Parnell's slow black talk poured molasses on every sentence. My God, it's confusing to be an immigrant. At the end of two months, I'd learned enough to hand my broom with the nail over to a new immigrant from Cuba. "Si senor."

I entered a cage full of red, yellow, and green parrots and was told to teach them something. Mrs. Moon looked over my shoulder and stuffed my pockets full of peanuts. "Make friends with them first." I wished I had entered a cage full of harpy eagles; with them I would have known exactly what to do.

With the macaws, I experimented and learned. I bought a kiddy slide, took my friendliest bird, and put him on the ground. He climbed up the side rail. I made it easier for him by covering the stairs with wire mesh. Now, he could climb in the middle. Result number one. He clamped his huge beak on the top part of the slide, one foot tentatively touching the slide. He slipped, squawked, and panicked. For two days he wouldn't go near the contraption. When he relaxed, I reversed the procedure. I placed him on the slide, but only inches from the ground. He slid without a problem. Good boy: give him a peanut.

In four days, I could send him from a distance to the ladder. He would step on the slide, hesitant at first, then let go and whoosh to the ground. I had trained my first bird in America. I got in touch with Alex. He was in Pittsburgh, busing tables at a country club. "Brother, we must meet somehow," he wrote. I agreed. But where and how? Meanwhile, I kept working with the huge parrots. The owner trusted me enough to try my hand with a pair of hyacinth macaws, the largest, most elegant, and most expensive members of the parrot family. The prop shop made me a miniature Roman chariot. I coaxed one bird to pull and the other to ride as the warrior in the back. On the command "turn," the "horse" executed a smart ninety-degree turn and ended up at my feet.

I was getting ambitious. I designed a new aerial scene with a bird piloting a plane, and even found a role for a dog. I wanted Chardash to join me. The owner liked the bird part but nothing about the dog. All the birds in the park would be afraid of it, and he wanted a purely feathered show anyway. At this early stage, I realized that America is the land of private enterprise. Somehow I would have to find a place where I could keep a few animals of my own, starting with Chardash.

Alex wrote to me about an Audubon club where I could get a job and keep a dog. In September, I startled my host, Walter, Parnell, and Mrs. Moon. "I am leaving for the north." They all wished me luck, and I flew back to New York. The Audubon job didn't pan out. The manager told me that the position had been filled in the meantime. I rented a room on the west side of Manhattan near Riverside Drive. Nick and Maria lived two blocks away. They insisted that I was their guest for every meal of the day. And if I missed one, Nick chewed me out. But what was worse, I couldn't stand Maria's accusing look if I dared to buy a meal on the outside.

Nick also explained to me how important it is to hold a job for a beginner, almost any job. I got one washing dishes at Schraft's on the corner of Fifth Ave and 52nd St. "Keep it in mind," Nick hammered at me. "It's temporary until you find something better." In the meantime, washing dishes wasn't too bad. I had my meals free, and my weekly take-home pay still could buy me a pair of shoes. "In Hungary, most people had to work for two months for a pair of footgear." I kept telling myself. "But how many pairs of shoes can you wear?"

I put an ad in an outdoor magazine. "Dog trainer, falconer, etc. wants position." A hunting preserve in Florida answered. Small wage, free room, and good tips from the dog owners. Once more, I was on my way to Florida. This time by Greyhound to stretch my fast-melting funds. The owner of the reserve was a caricature of a redneck. His first instruction was about the black help. "Now, you hear, you treat them decent, but you never shake hands with them. And you never call them boys 'mister.'"

Yes, the Deep South of 1957 was a completely different world. And how we criticized South Africa! Then he showed me my accommodations: a camper shell, three feet high, with a mattress and a blanket. When dark came, I bent double and crawled into my hole, staring at the warped plywood ceiling. It took me about five minutes to make up my mind. The next morning, I was riding the Greyhound north again. Nick and Maria were a bit surprised to see me so soon but not too much. "Write it off to experience," he said.

New hope on the horizon. Two hours from New York City—a park called Birch Hill Game Farm. I landed a job as a caretaker and animal keeper. In a beautiful setting, the park had a large collection of deer, buffalo, llama, a lonesome kangaroo sharing his run with an emu, and a very badly designed concrete monstrosity of a bear pit that contained four American black bears. The sanitizing of this den was my first major task. Hercules had it easy. At least the horses in the Aegean stables wouldn't try to tear him apart. My predecessor quit because he was afraid of the inmates. I stuck a ladder down the pit and climbed down. I watched the bears narrowly, ready to zip back up that ladder at the slightest hint of aggression. The bears sniffed and snuffled about lethargically. They even yawned, with nothing on their minds but winter hibernation. I began to shovel. What an anticlimax.

In the winter the game park closed to the public, and the slopes were covered with artificial snow. In the afternoons and the evenings, I became one of the artificial snow makers. The technique was in its infancy. The hoses and blowers kept freezing up constantly, and when working, the results were more mounds of ice than snow. It was hard work every step of the way, but like all pioneering, it was also fun.

Spring arrived in upstate New York. I moved to a log cabin on top of the hill. The little cottage was hidden in a grove of pine trees, and when the last car-full of tourists rolled off the hill, the entire place became mine. The birdsong, the trees, and the deer grazing in the empty parking lot. I bought my first car, a sleek blue and white Studebaker. My first important step in becoming an American. A taste of freedom from being tied to one place and schedules of public transport.

I told the manager about my dog in Austria. "Why don't you bring her over," he said. "There's plenty of room here for one more animal." Chardash arrived soon after. She greeted me as if we had never been parted. Her looks and friendly and polite manners won everybody's heart, just like in Europe.

Tina Louise and my Vizsla, Chardash

There was a sportsmen's show nearby, the biggest event of the region, and the park always had an exhibit of birds and small animals. There was also a stage show. Rope tricks, tomahawk thrower, and Tex Barton with his wonder horse, Freddie. Why not Chardash? In two weeks, I put together a simple routine—part bird-dog, part trick-dog. Chardash had more showmanship on her worst day than I had on my best. She was a success. Her picture made the front page of the local papers. I sent a clipping home, and everybody thought, "The kid has arrived." It took me a lot of letters to explain that it's easier to get in the papers here, especially the locals, than it is in Hungary. But deep down I was quite satisfied with the results.

Alex came to visit me from Pittsburgh. We had a touching reunion, and before he left we found him a job on the posh end of Long Island as a sort of gamekeeper/dog trainer on a millionaire's estate. At least we were in the same state—a distance of about three hundred miles but closer than Pittsburgh. And he was working outdoors in pleasant surroundings. Often, we would meet in New York at the Paprika restaurant, plot our future, and dream about returning to movie work. But how?

The Manhattan Yellow Pages had everything, including animal agents. We visited all who would listen to us. The most interesting establishment was Animal Talent Scouts, owned by Loraine d'Essen, a former model and the author of the book *Kangaroo in the Kitchen*. She swore that Ivan Tors stole the title of his movie *Zebra in the Kitchen* from her. I must admit there was a certain resemblance. Loraine's place was in the basement of an old brownstone on the lower West Side. She shared her rooms with Lancelot the llama, Skipper the kangaroo, Pierre the scarlet macaw, and a conglomeration of dogs and a gaggle of house cats. On her wall, an impressive array of clippings and ads featuring her own achievements and those of her animals. Her star animal was a smiling greyhound—the bus company's mascot.

By West Coast standards, neither she nor her handlers could be called trainers, but she had a knack for getting along with animals and people. Her partner, and the owner of an animal farm in New Jersey, was Captain Volney Pfeiffer, the man whose parachute-jumping lion was once featured in Ripley's *Believe It or Not*. When I met the Captain, he was in his declining years, but he still moved like a huge jungle cat. He was the only one who could silently open the clanking wrought iron gate leading to the Animal Talent Scouts' basement. I asked him once how he did it. He just smiled and said, "The gate doesn't resist me."

Loraine would listen to my tales of past achievements but to get her confidence was something else. Years later, when I completed several jobs for her, she told me that anyone can claim to be an eagle, or dog, or cheetah trainer, even if they never walked a poodle on a leash. I was amazed, astonished. Why would anyone claim to be a trainer? Wouldn't he be found out the first time he tried to work anything? At that time, I hadn't met that strange creature, the animal phony. But it didn't take me very long to get acquainted with this not-so-rare breed. Chardash and Loraine got me my first job on American television. It was a dog-food commercial for Gravy Train. The story-board called for the dog running on a narrow jetty and diving from about three feet into the lake. With lots of enthusiasm and without a second's hesitation, because nothing, but nothing, will keep Barbra the Swimmingest Dog out of the water, except, of course, the magic words shouted by a divine voice: "Graaavy Traaaain."

I visited the location a few days before shooting and knew I had no problems. She dove off the board after a ball or a stick, and on the first call she turned and headed for shore, just like the script demanded. Loraine said that was fine; she'll make a good backup dog, but this is such an important client that, for dog number one, she had booked a Hollywood wonder canine called Mister Trouble. As long as we get paid, I said, Chardash can be number two or number three or any number. Neither her feelings nor mine will be hurt.

On the day of the shoot, I showed up in my stylish old Studebaker. Mister Trouble and his owners showed up in an air-conditioned Cadillac. That dog did amazing tricks. On cue, he yawned, limped, closed his left eye. And I felt very, very, superfluous. This lasted until eleven o'clock that morning when we discovered the limit of the wonder dog's powers. Diving off a board just wasn't in his repertoire. Mister Trouble would walk at a medium speed to the edge, wag his tail, look back at his owner, and perhaps even shrug his shoulders. His look seemed to say, "You want me to jump in this water? It isn't even chlorinated, much less heated." The trainer tried everything: the stern approach, the gentle approach, the pleading to his better nature approach. Boredom and frustration spread throughout the set. Finally, somebody remembered, "Don't we have a double dog?" Chardash sauntered out with me, confident, glad to have something to do at last. She was a beautiful dog, with the fluid grace of all Vizslas—and their love of water. She dove for the long shot. She dove for the medium shot and then for all the close-ups.

TC Just stood there shaking his head. This was breaking his heart. During lunch, he took the disgraced Mister Trouble on a leash and walked him onto the plank. He spoke quietly and sternly. "So help me," he told the mutt, "this is how you do it." At that, the frustrated animal trainer dove head first into the water. He came to the surface spluttering, his cheeks strangely drawn. He looked as if he'd seen a ghost down there in the murky waters. What really happened was that he had lost his dentures somewhere at the bottom of the lake. Mister Trouble wagged his tail and smiled. That was some smart dog.

I felt sorry for my fellow trainer and kept searching on the muddy bottom until I found his choppers. Chardash and I drove home with the warm glow of accomplishment. From this day on I had Lorraine's confidence. Chardash did several more commercials and the print ads that appeared in *Life* magazine. But these were still all part time jobs. I was still a full time keeper at Birch Hill, but I felt we had started on the way back to the movies. Next year, at the Sportsman's Show, Zippy the chimp was the featured star. A very entertaining, fast moving, ape that did his whole act on roller skates. If I had lost my job at Birch Hill to Zippy I would have bowed my head to someone who was my superior. Instead, I lost my job to the first animal phony I met. He owned a pet shop and had a baby chimp in his arms. He told the president of the park "Next year, I will have my chimp roller skating like Zippy." The manager wanted to keep me. The president wanted the future roller skating ape. The president won. So far, I had quit three times and got fired once.

Alex took Chardash to Long Island, and I got a job as a veterinarian's kennel help. His practice included a small wild animal collection of Millbrook College. This group of animals was the pride and joy of the biology professor, Frank Trevor. In my new job I cleaned and fed the feline and canine patients. Assisted with the operations, mostly spaying and castration. The cat castrations shocked me a bit. Dr. B was a good vet but on the frugal side. More than that, he felt that the price of the anesthesia was better in his pocket. The tomcats were wrapped in a towel; two fast slits of a scalpel and tom was a eunuch. Just before the owner showed up, Dr. B sprayed a drop of ether on the morose patient's fur. The owners never knew better.

I liked it better at Birch Hill, but the main thing is to have a job. I kept telling myself it was temporary. Half a year later, Birch Hill was looking for a new keeper. The part pet shop owner, part chimp educator didn't work out. I was still sore at the president, and I'm sure he was sore at me. But I managed to get the job for Alex. Now we lived only forty-five minutes from each other.

Alex met Breda, a lovely Irish girl. I wrote a letter to her parents in his name asking for her hand. Considering he only had two and a half years of schooling—or more exactly basic training—in his own language, Alex's English was quite adequate, especially when it came to business dealings. But spelling he never mastered, so not surprisingly I became his ghostwriter. The answer was yes from the Emerald Isle. Alex and Breda were married in New York City. I was the best man, naturally. What a combination: fiery Irish and headstrong Hungarian. But Alex was beaming with happiness, and his bride was beautiful, as all brides are. This event was followed by nuptials for Chardash. Alex found a mate for her, and she had six golden-rust velvety pups. Being a refugee, she had no papers. Four of the pups we gave away. Alex kept the feisty little runt of the group. He named it Rajko (pronounced Ryko), which means "gypsy brat" in Hungarian. I kept a big-boned sturdy pup and named him Amber.

At Birch Hill, we could keep some of our own animals, and at Henry Trefflich's place on Canal Street, we bought a perky little lioness. We named her Sabor, after the lioness in the Tarzan books. For better or worse, the animal dealer's store is now a part of history, but it was then as much a part of New York as the Fulton Fish Market. On any given day, one could find baby gorillas or orangs playing with tiger or leopard cubs in Henry's window, next to the more familiar fare of guinea pigs, chihuahuas, or parrots. It was such a short time ago, and yet it seems like fiction now. Henry went out of business thirty years ago, a victim of changing attitudes, laws, and the worldwide disappearance of wildlife.

Sabor, Rajko, and Amber had an ideal time growing up at Birch Hill. During the day, they were the star attraction at the animal nursery under Chardash's motherly supervision. The evenings were fun time. Playing a game called "butt biters," lion cub or pup would hide behind a clump of grass or convenient bush and pounce on a playmate from behind, then run as fast as their short legs could carry them. Rajko was the undisputed butt-biting champion.

Only at feeding time did Sabor assert herself as the queen. She clamped her oversize paws around the dish, and if any of the dogs approached, she curled her lips, showing needle sharp baby teeth. A surprisingly deep rumble warned a trespasser to keep his distance. Sabor also took solo walks on her own. One second she would be sleeping on the porch, and the next she vanished. At first we worried about her getting lost, but she always showed up before dark. What she did on these solitary excursions, we never knew. According to Alex, she was looking at the horses at the nearby riding stable trying to decide which one to catch next year. This was sometime before Elsa, the heroine of *Born Free*, captured the heart of the world. Sabor's childhood was an upstate New York variation of her famous relative's story. By the time she was a year old she weighed 150 pounds, and when she ran at full speed the ground fairly shook under her huge paws. In the winter we took her for short walks. She loved to roll in the snow, her steamy breath pouring from her pink mouth and extended nostrils.

For a while life was idyllic at Birch Hill, but somehow life always changes. The animal business is strictly for those who love insecurity or at least can cope with it. The good news was that, after five years as a resident alien, I became an American citizen, a member of the best country the world ever knew or will know. Born in Hungary of a Bavarian father, I now felt as American as apple pie. For the bad news, business started to fall off at Birch Hill and my vet's office at the same time. His large animal practice was profitable, but not the small animal clientele. Perhaps one of the towel-castrated tomcats squealed on him or the competition did it. Alex and I lost our jobs the same week in the spring of 1962. We had to find a home for Sabor. She went to the Warwick Game farm, and I never saw her again, but she kindled a flame in my heart for the African lion that has kept on burning ever since.

I became night watchman at Millbrook College. From 10 p.m. till 6 a.m., I walked my rounds with a time clock around my neck, visiting the fourteen strategic points around the sleeping campus. During the Cuban missile crisis, I felt very important, scanning the southern skies for Kruschev's rockets. The only spectacular firework I witnessed was provided by nature and came from the north: the eerie display of northern lights, rare in upstate New York. The silent, scanning, yellow-green shafts reminded me of the searchlights during the war.

But these were manned by elves or by King Arthur's wicked fairy sister, Morgan le Fay.

Alex bought a house and started to deal in ornamental pheasants and other small game. Unlike myself, he always had a knack for horse-trading. Back in Hungary, he supplied the film with pigeons for our birds of prey. There was an old homing pigeon he sold to Comrade Director at least six times. "Take the ring off his foot," Adam warned him, "before someone notices the miraculous return of Boomerang"—as the old bird was named.

The job of night watchman had its advantages. If I didn't insist on sleeping, the daytime hours were mine. A rodeo trainer, Tex Barton, suggested I run a nightclub act. I came up with the idea of Amber and a leopard working together. I reasoned that a leopard was the only big cat I could control myself without backup from other trainers. Henry Trefflich's store was my source once more. Out of a litter of three Indian leopard cubs, I picked the brightest pale-blue-eyed charmer. Nabokov's teenage vamp was the most popular heroine of the day, and somehow the sensuous name of Lolita fitted the spotted ball of fur. She rode home with me in the back of my Studebaker.

Frank, my professor mentor, let me keep her at the college zoo, together with Amber, who had by now become a handsome, muscular retriever. At nights when the campus slept, the three of us kept the peace on the grounds. Only the headmaster's cat did not like the dog and leopard patrol. He sat on the entrance column spitting at the three of us.

Lolita working

A living fur collar

Animal talent scouts used Lolita for a perfume ad with Sophia Loren. It was Lolita's first job, and she performed like a pro. However, the famous Italian beauty was extremely nervous of her co-star. She wanted the session to be over as soon as possible. I have the greatest respect for the acting class; it is a difficult profession. When the cold lens of the camera focuses on you, something frightening happens. An actor has only one commodity to sell: himself. For many, even other humans hardly exist. An animal is a prop at best, competition at worst. There are exceptions, like Errol Flynn, who respected animals and their trainers, but this observation is the general rule.

On Lolita's first birthday, I started to train my act. For a third member, I added Sapphire, a blue and gold macaw. What made my efforts unusual was the compatibility of dog and leopard. In the wild, the leopard's favorite food is monkeys and canines. There are several cases on record when Mr. Spots leaped through an open window and departed with Fido in his jaws without so much as waking the owner. I emphasized comedy in my act. For instance, Amber is on one pedestal and the leopard on the other. Lolita leaps, knocking Amber off his seat. Amber runs and jumps on Lolita's vacant platform. The big cat jumps and bumps him off again. But enough is enough: the dog grabs the leopard's tail to hold her down, then jumps up next to her and clamps his jaws around the cat's mouth—a variation on the old trainer in the lion's maw routine.

For my big finale, I did the leopard merry-go-round. Holding Lolita by the front paws, I swung her around, and with the momentum of the final arc, I would fling her upon my shoulder. Draped in living leopard, I would salute regally and exit. My trial audience, the students at the college, appreciated my trio. I was ready with my small menagerie to hit the road.

I traded my faithful Studebaker for a bulky but useful station wagon, the green giant, and bought a small trailer. In November 1963, I gathered all my belongings, said farewell to the college, and Alex. He looked at me with the look of those who stay behind. He had new responsibilities. Breda was expecting her first child.

Bookings are for the pessimistic and the well organized. I had faith in the unusual combination of my companions, and with the security of $600, my life savings, in my pocket, I kept on rolling south. Through Washington DC, still mourning our assassinated young president, through the Carolinas, the red silt of Georgia (the land of Scarlett O'Hara). In three days I found myself in Silver Springs, Florida, home of glass-bottomed boats, gift shops galore, Bartlett's Deer Farm, and Ross Allen's Reptile Institute. I knew Ross Allen as one of the great names in the field of exploring, animal collecting, and as a top expert of venomous creepy-crawlies. Of all his credits, the most impressive was his role as stunt double for my childhood jungle hero, Johnny Weissmuller, the king of all movie Tarzans.

Most of the underwater crocodile and giant snake fights were staged in the crystal clear pools of Silver Springs. And when it came time to replace the rubber croc with a live alligator or anaconda, it was Ross who put on the loincloth and Lord Greystoke's hunting knife and fought the water-churning battle. An exceptionally belligerent anaconda nearly kept him down for the fatal count, and Weissmuller himself came to the rescue, peeling off the coils of the giant constrictor. The Reptile Institute displayed a large collection of snakes and amphibians with an alligator show and rattlesnake venom milking demonstration. At times, the master himself would do the show, and rumor has it a playful mc, either as a slip of the tongue or just being hilarious, announced, "And now ladies and gentlemen, Ross Allen is going to milk himself." The boss didn't think it was funny and fired the joker on the spot. Ross and I hit it off from the beginning. I showed my talented trio to him, and he hired us for the winter season. That was fine by me. April seemed a long way away, and I had a place for the cold months.

I worked my act between the alligator show and the venom extraction four times a day. Sue Ellen, a tall blonde divorcee in the gift shop, posed with Lolita for a postcard. We became friends and took trips on our days off. Where else but to other Florida tourist attractions? At Web City, the largest drugstore in the world, I got a booking for two weeks in May. Ross Allen introduced me to the best-known trainer of all times, the legendary Clyde Beatty. It was like a small parish priest meeting the pope. The preeminent lion-tamer of movies and the circus ring for forty years, Clyde is the only trainer to have made the cover of *Time* magazine. His specialty was the old-fashioned fighting act. Lots of noise, snarling, pouncing, whip cracking, and blanks fired mostly for the audience's benefit.

His long pliant whip was for cuing and showmanship. For protection, he used the light chair unique to the American big cat trainers. The way he explained it to me, and before me to Ernest Hemingway, "This prop serves the same function as the bullfighter's muleta. It draws the animal's attention. The four legs offer a confusing choice—which one do I bite first?" His chairs were reinforced with bolts at every joint and pressure point. Ordinary screws couldn't stand the stormy battering of giant paws. Even with special strengthening, his chairs didn't last very long. He was a good customer for the bentwood furniture industry.

I watched him practice a new "gate-crusher" for the finale of his act. All the cats had done their stuff and were sent home, except for the biggest, most menacing, black-maned lion. Clyde stood in the middle of the arena, chair and whip on defensive alert. The big feline went into a menacing half-crouch and circled him the way any cat circles a mouse. At the right moment, Beatty threw down his chair and whip, turned his back on the lion and ran. The second the chair hit the ground, Black Mane was after him. Beatty's refuge was a small four-foot square safety cage at the edge of the arena. The same instant the door slammed shut, Black Mane was at the bars, rampant like a heraldic beast, towering over the short, stocky man. His claws raked the air inches from the face of this master showman on the other side of the bars.

I showed Beatty my hound and leopard in their small trailer. He smiled and said he might cut his act down to this size one day. I got bold and asked him if he would consider me to take over when he retired. (Ross Allen had told me he was contemplating hanging up his whip and chair.) "Can you crack a whip?" he asked. Of course, in my act I used a modified horse crop with lash and popper. It gave some seriousness to the mostly comic happenings. And in Hungary, I learned to crack the long, plaited whips of our herdsmen. Full of confidence, I took my whip out of the trailer, assumed the proper stance, wound up, and brought the lash back. But instead of the loud crack I heard only a humiliating "pfftt!" Lolita had chewed the popper off the end. Now I felt like the village chaplain who forgot the words to the "Our Father" before the pope. Clyde suppressed a smile, and I could see he wasn't impressed.

"I'm taking the show on the road soon. Meet me in New York, and we'll work out a plan. In the meantime, practice with your whip," he added with a wink. But I never saw Clyde Beatty again. Six months later he departed for that big arena in the sky. "I expect one of these days they are going to get me," he would say about his jungle adversaries, partners, and friends. But they never did. Instead the Big C, throat cancer, brought to dust the greatest showman of the American Big Top. Our few meetings and his kindness to an acolyte like me will always occupy a special corner on the shelf of my memories.

At the end of March, I headed back to New York. Lorraine was looking for a sea lion trainer for an upcoming Broadway musical, *Fade Out – Fade In*, starring Carol Burnett. Sea mammals were a new kettle of fish. But why not? Adam's words rang in my ear, "If it walks, flies, or swims, don't turn it down. You can, you must, handle it." Smaxi was the star of the Philadelphia aquarium. He applauded, rolled over, did flipper stands and many other amusing tricks. I said tricks, and I know that the politically correct word these days is behaviors. But I'm old-fashioned. If "tricks" was good enough for Clyde Beatty, it's good enough for me. Anyway, "stupid pet behaviors" doesn't sound quite right.

Carol Burnett and Smaxi the sea lion

Fade Out – Fade In was a flashy musical. Dancing girls on a giant piano and catchy tunes written for the comic talents of Ms. Burnett. She played a wide-eyed usherette summoned to Hollywood by misplaced identity, gets the role, loses the role to luck and talent, retrieves the role, and becomes a star. If it sounds simple, it was. The audience loved it, and it played to full houses every night. The story took place at FFF Studios where Smaxi was the seal of approval and mascot a la MGM lion. If a new actor or actress was liked by him, he shook hands, and the part was automatically hers. But if Smaxi refused to offer his flipper, that was also automatically a one-way ticket back to Lower Sandusky or wherever the applicant came from. Smaxi loved Carol but refused to shake hands with her rival, the gorgeous Tina Louise.

He had his dressing room with a portable pool at the Mark Hellinger Theater, received his five-minute warning like the rest of the cast. No matter how many times I changed his water, his room and the entire floor always gave out a heavy bouquet of eau de mackerel. Some of the finicky choirboys objected to his aroma, but that was their problem. Smaxi was the star, and as an actor, he didn't stink at all. In May, I had to return to Web City and do my two-week stint with Lolita and Amber. I handed Smaxi over to one of Lorraine's keepers. By now he was such a trouper, he worked for anyone who had a bucket of fish.

I collected my act from Alex and drove to St. Pete. Between performances, I took long swims in the Gulf of Mexico. It happened here that a *Life* photographer tracked me down for a layout about the unusual relationship between my dog and leopard. Normally, one the consumer, one the consumee. For some reason, the reporter made up the story that the three of us go hunting along the Silver River. But what do we hunt? I borrowed a scared possum from Ross Allen. I didn't know exactly how the leopard would react, but soon found out. She was indifferent—if anything a bit worried. I baited her with bits of meat to get her near the supposed victim. The possum performed the role nature intended for him, and the photographer got the desired shots. The rest of the shoot was pure fun. Amber and Lolita gamboled among the tropical plants and even took an unexpected plunge in the river. We recreated the dog pulling the leopard's tail on a stump. When published, this shot opened the article. The snarling little opossum never made it into *Life* magazine.

I hoped that after a three-page exposure in the world's most prestigious magazine, offers would start pouring in. But our fan mail consisted of one single letter asking me if Lolita's unusually large rosettes were hiding a jaguar in leopard's clothing. My big break came from a different direction. At the end of an afternoon show, a gentleman stepped out of the crowd and introduced himself as Henry S., a director and producer for the Walt Disney Studios.

Henry was filming nearby with a stallion and a jaguar from Hollywood. The horse being the star and the jaguar the menace. Or, according to the director, more like aggravation, grief, and lost production time. He was impressed with the instant response from my animals and asked if I could stop for a chat on his location on my way north. Would I? Could I? Nobody could stop me. After six years, I finally get to see a proper movie set. I turned Amber and Lolita loose, let them play, jump, and climb to their hearts' content. Henry liked what he saw and told me there was definitely a script in the friendship of these animals. I agreed wholeheartedly but didn't get my hopes up too high.

In New York, I took Smaxi back and appeared nightly as Joe the Seal trainer in *Fade Out – Fade In*. Weeks passed, and I almost forgot about my brief meeting with Hollywood when I received a letter from Disney Studios. A script has been written and approved, featuring my leopard and retriever, and how soon can I come? As soon as I come back from Europe, I answered. The political climate after four years of terror and retaliation had improved in Hungary. Protected behind the blue cover of my American passport and citizenship, I made plans to visit my relatives and friends in the old country. "Have a good trip," came the reply from Henry. "We'll see you, animals and all, in sunny California at the end of September."

After seven years of absence, I landed on Austrian soil. The three of us—Rita, Imre, and I—caught up on the flow of our lives. Imre finished his studies and was working for a Vienna firm as an engineer building roads and bridges. Rita was delighted to see me and listened to my struggles and occasional success in far-off America. In a couple of days, we puttied the cracks of missing years. I rented an Opel Cadet and headed for the same border I crossed so illegally in 1957. American passport or not, every kilometer that got me closer to the real Iron Curtain cut the stomach wound tighter and tighter. I fully realized once I crossed the barbed wire, I was at the mercy of the system. Nobody would start World War III over my disappearance. It seemed as if my car stood still and the massive red, white, and green barrier kept creeping inexorably closer. An invisible power raised it like an invitation to walk into the dragon's den. Somebody's foot, it couldn't possibly be mine, stepped on the gas. My car rolled forward, and I was back in Hungary. Silently, the thick iron arm lowered. It was too late to back out. A tank couldn't bust through it. And that was the very idea.

A polite but cool border guard took my passport and disappeared behind a solid iron door. I stood leaning on my car, trying to concentrate on the sound of the meadowlark and not the baying of the Dobermans in the kennels. Forty-five minutes later, the keeper of the frontier handed me my precious travel document. The second massive barrier in front of me was raised and, relieved, I started my journey inland.

My visit was a surprise. Good news never killed anybody. The family was at the lakeside villa. For the next two weeks, I was the returning prodigal son. The small cottage overflowed with the aroma of my favorite dishes, and hearts glowed with love saved up for seven long years.

I went to see Adam, Comrade Director, his wife Eva—still a spectacular, if a bit zaftig, lady. Of the stars of *Pals*, the dachshund Gossip was dead. And Chum the retriever was just hanging on. Almost completely deaf, his once beautiful golden rust coat had turned mousey gray; he tiredly wagged his tail as I petted his wrinkled head.

Adam had two fascinating birds. Witch was a Peregrine falcon with a story. She was a native of Siberia, where a trigger-happy shootist sprayed her with shotgun pellets. She survived and wound up at the Moscow zoo. Later she was traded for the Old One, our male cheetah. Between two fraternal socialist countries, it was considered a fair trade. Witch could never be returned to the wild, but Adam kept mending and exercising her injured wing until she could take to the sky once more, nearly perfect. Only an expert eye could tell she tilted to the left.

The other bird was Edgar. Raven by species, clown by profession. When I first saw him, he was occupied with a huge stag beetle. The male of these insects is equipped with pincers two to three inches long and can grab a finger or a fresh raven's beak with considerable strength. This specimen was lying on his back—tits up, as the cowboys say—but Edgar had to make sure that his lunch would not object. He waddled over to the hedge and returned with a dry twig. Cautiously, he hopped to the dead bug, head cocked, ready to jump. Then he dropped the branch on his intended meal. When it didn't move, he picked it up and dissected it with the precision of a coroner.

I coveted both birds instantly, and Adam was willing to part with them. But he foresaw problems. "If you take them as a falcon and a raven, the government will see dollar signs flashing, and the red tape of the Reds will keep you here to Christmas." I couldn't do that. Across the ocean, in California, Mr. Disney was waiting for me. "On the other hand, goshawks and crows are a dime a dozen. Are you willing to take the chance that at the border you won't run into an ex-game warden who can tell the difference?" Chance taking is my middle name, and at the end of my visit I rolled into Austria with Edgar and Witch riding on the back seat of the Opel Cadet. Seems like I just can't leave the old country lawfully. I always have to smuggle something out.

In New York, Breda met me at the airport with the unpleasant news that Alex was in bed with ulcers. Nothing serious, just unpleasant and surprising. He seemed to have the indestructible constitution of a bison and now the first attack of ulcers. The sight of Witch and Edgar and the letter I hand-carried from his parents made him feel better.

CHAPTER 8

HOORAY FOR HOLLYWOOD: ALSO FOR BURBANK

t was time to pack up my worldly belongings, but this time I did it full of hope. The green giant station wagon and the light trailer could still hold all my possessions and my animals. Lolita and Amber in the trailer, Chardash next to me on the passenger side. Following old Route 66, the trail west, I avoided regular rest stops and managed to find a dirt road or abandoned farm building to clean and feed my traveling companions. After Chicago, I even found open spaces to fly Witch.

It was late September when I crossed the California border at Needles. It was easy to see why the conquistadors called it *caliente fornalia*, hot furnace. The searing heat of the Santa Ana winds pushed us a day later to the promised land of Hollywood and Burbank, where Disney Studios is located. Henry and his surprised family put up my collection in the garage of their suburban home. The screech of the falcon and macaw raised a few curious eyebrows among the neighbors. I felt relieved when we left Los Angeles and arrived on location at the foot of the western Sierras, below the Sequoia National Park.

"Who is going to be your assistant?" asked Henry. Well, I just happen to know a fellow in New York. A week later, Alex, his family, and his favorite animals followed me to the golden land of California. His collection included Rajko, Amber's brother; a spider monkey; a slightly deranged stump-tail macaque named Fingers; and Hannibal, a Barbary sheep, or aoudad, from the Atlas Mountains of North Africa. Alex got him as part of his back wages from Birch Hill Game Farm. We called him the only trained aoudad in the world. He jumped a hurdle on cue, stood on his hind legs, and nibbled carrots from his trainer's mouth. Not an earth-shaking routine but more than the average aoudad does.

Every film production has a gag or saying that is repeated until it dies of overuse. On *Pals* the slogan was "Up to new idiocies." On *A Zoo in My Backyard*, our current epic, "How is your aoudad?" became our motto. During the '60s, most children grew up with Lassie and the Sunday program of Disney's *Wonderful World of Color*. *Backyard Zoo* was planned to be one of these pearls. On these shows, the story seldom changed; the animals did. The hero was perhaps a coyote with super human intelligence or a skunk that only sprayed bad guys or a goose that walked across the country to meet his mate.

Backyard Zoo was different. It had several different animal heroes. A leopard (Lolita) code-named Shandy. Amber and Rajko playing the feral dog Duke. In supporting roles, a motley group of mutts under the leadership of a strange mongrel with the androgynous name of Shirley Sean. His name might have been a bit sissy, but in body and heart Shirley Sean was 100 percent macho. He was a born hobo, ugly as sin, with a gray-brown wiry coat and clashing light blue and brown eyes. He was bumming around town, never staying too long at any one house. Of course, he got the blame for all the missing cats. Shirley, the owner of the ranch where we stayed, asked me if I'd take him before some resentful farmer sank a handful of buckshot in his breeches. We gave him a screen test, and when those mismatched eyes looked at us from the screen we knew we had found a hero.

Fingers, Alex's lunatic monkey, supplied the story's comic relief. At regular intervals he'd go into a spastic routine of counting his fingers. First on his hands, then on his feet. A frozen stare alternating with a torrent of monkey gibberish as he admired his digits. He'd go on for minutes until, as suddenly as it came, the attack stopped. Steven, our cameraman, needed super-human control to keep his machine from shaking while he filmed this performance. The rest of us rolled on the ground with aching sides.

Fingers, the neurotic monkey

How did an exotic menagerie end up taking place in northern California? Easy. That's what script-writers are for. A young widow buys a cottage sight unseen in the foothills. One of those fixer-uppers where a box of nails and a bucket of paint can work wonders. So far the story is familiar and it keeps getting more familiar. The truck of a traveling showman, "Gypsy Joe," takes a curve too fast. He ends up in a ditch, and his animals melt into the pine and manzanite jungle.

Sally, our heroine, who by now has turned her rundown shack into a neat gingerbread, is also known to have a way with animals. She helps the sheriff collect the vagrant group of aoudad, monkeys, falcon, and, as the danger music swells, Shandy the leopard. Henry picked local talent for the smaller parts, but the character of Sally called for a professional actress. Susanna was tall and blonde, and her husband had a job with the Air Force. When I looked at her, I sighed at the heavens. Why couldn't I meet someone as serious as Susanna? When the gods want to punish you...!

We filmed at a slow but exacting pace. Time did not seem to matter as long as we delivered the exact footage demanded by the studio. If Mr. Disney wanted the aoudad to enter from camera left, sniff at a daisy, then look to camera with a puzzled expression, we were expected to deliver that footage, if not this week, the next.

All productions have a reoccurring event, or curse. On this one we had a curse of escaping animals. First was Witch, my beautiful, reliable falcon from Siberia. On a foggy afternoon, I was flying her in the valley. Not the best terrain for a bird from the open steppes. At the end of the exercise, she tried to land on a telephone pole, and her talons slipped on the insulator. Unbalanced, she took off in a narrow canyon. My calls remained unanswered. There are few things more foolish and depressing than a falconer returning at the end of the day with an empty glove.

The next day, Alex joined the search without any results, but the day after, at sunrise, she was sitting on her perch screaming at me as if the whole incident had been my fault.

For the next great escape, Sally's five movie dogs dug out of the kennel, under the leadership of that reformed vagabond Shirley Sean. By noon, four of them trotted home contrite and muddy, but Andy the Afghan hound started to play games. He stood just outside the compound with a grin on his fox-like face.

"Here I am. Come and get me." When we approached, he loped away sideways like a huge crab, keeping a tantalizing ten feet between us. Alex had a brilliant idea. The rancher next door, Skinny Kirk, had a beagle bitch just dying to become a mother. We borrowed her and tied her in the middle of the compound. Andy was interested but not enough to enter. Alex stayed up all night holding a long rope attached to the gate and, around midnight, finally recaptured the fugitive.

In the movie, Alex played a fisherman who recaptures Gypsy Joe's wild sheep, Hannibal. Obeying the first rule of all film animals—turn your ass to the camera—Hannibal did just that, dropped a few sheep pellets for us, and jumped on a rock in the river. Soon he was grazing on the opposite shore on fragrant wild grass. He was missing for three days, and we all started to get nervous, and Henry's quips did not help my confidence much. Shirley Sean saved the day. He cornered the fugitive in a cul-de-sac until Alex could get a rope on him. But all these adventures were just a warm up to the most serious escape of all.

We were filming a simple A to B with Lolita when a wild rabbit popped up in front of her nose. The temptation was too much. She ran after the bunny. Rabbit and leopard headed for an old barbed-wire fence. Lolita ran into the wire, scraped her back, and the panic switch was thrown; a loud frightened grunt and she was gone. Naturally, all filming stopped. We spread out, calling and searching for the fugitive. To find a needle in a haystack is relatively easy compared to a leopard that doesn't want to be found. There is a saying among the professional hunters of Africa: "Put a match box on a billiard table, and a leopard will hide behind it." The foothills of the Sierras offered considerably more hiding places than a matchbox.

I hoped she would find me when she was ready. I sent everybody home and with Amber, her canine friend, settled down on a flat rock for a long wait. The hours moved with the slowness of cooling lava, and I had plenty to think about. It was a wild area; the nearest ranch was at least ten miles away. Even if she met an adult, she would not attack. Small children were another matter. I watched a pair of golden eagles sailing on the thermals of noonday heat, and I sent a silent wish to them: "Birds, if you see an overgrown spotted cat . . . let me know." Early afternoon came and still no sign of Lolita. Amber perked up his ears and raised my heartbeat, but it was only a rattlesnake sneaking by on last year's dry leaves. An hour before sunset and the shadows were stretching closer to my rock. Suddenly Amber sat up, and at the edge of the thicket, where a second ago there was only grass, stood my jungle cat, lonely and insecure. I send the dog. He bounds up to his friend; she rubs her face against him and, as if nothing has happened, walks up to me. The relief felt at a moment like this is almost worth the agony. But only almost.

Leopard and Vizsla

Hubby's visits to our leading lady became less and my dates with Susanna more frequent. An Eastern sage said men are always looking for adventure, and women are looking for love. Most of the time women find adventure only, and if a man finds love it scares him. Like most affairs, it started as just fun. Dinner conversations about her travel to Japan, and I told tales of my spoiled but amazing childhood in Europe. Then we spent the first night together. It was a small town, and tongues started to wag with the speed of summer lightning. I always felt that the saying "no man is an island" did not apply to me: if I was an island, I welcomed visitors but no settlement allowed. She wanted more and more of my time, and we had our first fight. I walked on the wrong side of the street. She reminded me that a gentleman always takes the street side. She took my answer as flippant and tore into me, eyes flashing.

The next day, she did not show up on the set, and the director asked me to get her by deeds, promises, or whatever. "She'll come back to you, like Lolita," grinned Alex. We made up, and our stormy relationship lasted for six years. But as time passed our relationship became more and more stormy. Finally, all I asked for was to at least not fight in public. She agreed. A few days later, I looked at a passing blonde two seconds longer than I should have. She left four long scratch marks on my face. The location made it more public. It happened in front of NBC Studios, and the long line of tourists waiting for the *Tonight Show* thought it was part of the pre-show entertainment. To make matters worse, the next day I had to be on camera as a nineteenth-century seal trainer with Rex Harrison as the original Dr. Dolittle. The make-up man had quite a job to fill in the gashes.

Of course, we had lots of marvelous times as well, but I always felt I was wired to a time bomb, and she was in control of the switch. If I did not show up at her house, she'd call the studio and promise calmness. Being a weak man, I gave in, and as I entered she flew at me for not taking my shoes off. The end was as stormy as the rest of our relationship. I was half an hour late for a date. I apologized and got into her car. She took off with silent rage on her beautiful face.

"I am taking you to the insane asylum in Camarillo. A person like you belongs no other place."

If I am crazy I might as well act it. I grabbed the wheel and forced the car across two lanes of traffic to the curb. There is never a policeman around when you need one. I did not need one right now, but there was one right on our tail. I ended up with heaviest, most deserved fine of my life. But the wildest and deepest relationship of my life was finally over. At least until I got married. The next time we met was at Alex's funeral, and we finally became good friends who care but do not demand or interfere. In retrospect it was probably worth it, but never again. One fatal attraction is enough in any man's life, never mind two.

My first American movie was finished, but my contact with Henry became slightly strained, and who could blame him? What transpired between the leading lady and myself was not exactly a director's dream. For his next show, he used Alex only, and I was with my animals, as the saying goes "between engagements." In show biz, one is never unemployed, but the results are the same. The money is going out and nothing is coming in.

CHAPTER 9

ONCE THERE WAS A PLACE CALLED JUNGLELAND

I n the '60s, there were two major companies providing animals for films. The upstart Africa U.S.A. was under the stewardship of Ivan Tors. Ivan was responsible for Daktari, Flipper, and similar fares on the tube. He was a kindly man with rather bad taste who made a fortune in movies without actually making one good film. He was also a fellow Hungarian so I am allowed to criticize him. The other establishment, Jungleland, was the granddad of all movie compounds. I was turned down for employment at Africa U.S.A. A bit reluctantly, I showed up at Jungleland and was hired on the spot thanks to my dog and leopard act. The place was old, and it showed. If someone invented a machine to neutralize bailing wire, the place would have fallen apart, but in the old pens the animals were well cared for, and it was a dream place to meet the legends of the training profession.

FRIENDLY TIGER—Mel Koontz poses with Satan, a full grown Sumatran tiger which he trained from the time it was three weeks old. Satan was the first tiger to appear in films requiring contact with other actors.

Melvin Koontz, the idol of movie trainers

Melvin Koontz was the pioneer of big cats used in movies, and we who came after him, including myself, should be honored to wipe his seat. He was a specialist who handled nothing but lions, tigers, leopards, and cougars. Satan, Mel's best wrestling tiger, was a Sumatran, a subspecies with a reputation for being tough and insecure. The term "wrestling cat" or "hit cat" in the trainer's jargon means a feline that can do a simulated attack or kill, and the human can walk away when the director yells "Cut." A tiger mauling a gladiator, a lion flattening Tarzan, is a wrestling cat. In a scene like this, the trainer plays with the animal's killing instinct and, observing the safety rules, controls it. In these episodes the trainer always doubles the actor.

As long as man stands up, he is unique. Our silhouette is different from all other animals, but when knocked down and lying on the ground, the equation changes, and you had better be on excellent terms with the three hundred or five hundred pounds of jungle muscle straddling you. On one occasion Melvin wrestled Satan with his broken leg in a cast and hobbled away without a scratch. His most famous animal was Jackie the lion. Actually, there were Jackie Number One, Jackie Number Two, and Jackie Number Three, but Number One was by far the best. In an old movie, if you see Laurel and Hardy, Harold Lloyd, or a jungle epic and a scraggly-maned lion with a face only a lioness can love, that is Jackie Number One. An ugly cat but a great performer and trainer. Old stagehands ask me when I work a lion, "Is this Jackie?" My reply is, "I wish."

Johnny Weissmuller could actually take the first part of the charge still standing, but when it came to the knockdown, Mel always doubled for him.

In one of the stories I heard about Jackie Number One, the director wanted the lion to look dead with a spear in his side. A scene already made complicated with a makeup wound and fake blood. When Jackie complied, the director had an afterthought: "Now make him twitch his hind foot." When all else failed, cussing him out helped, Melvin told me. That's what he did now. "Move your leg, you hairy old son of a bitch." And slowly the hind leg moved. The director stood there with tears in his eyes not believing what he saw. Melvin was rather loud and vulgar in a good-natured way, and when he took the leash off Jackie, Satan, or some other cat, there was only one boss on the set: him.

He was filming with Cecil B. DeMille. After a satisfactory take, the director burst out as they often do. "That was great. I loved it. Now let's do one just like it. "

"If you liked it so much, why don't you print the son of a bitch twice? Me and my cat are going home."

"But Mr. Koontz, be reasonable," pleaded the director.

"I don't have to be reasonable, I am Melvin Koontz."

For a long time, I had an urge to try this line someday, probably the week I retired; I'd say, "Mr. Coppola or Mr. Pollack, I don't have to be reasonable, I am H.G. Wells." I'd probably get as far as the studio gate with that line.

In *Demetrius and the Gladiators* Mel was doubling for Victor Mature in the tiger attack scene. Satan was in a playful mood and jumped so high he ended up on top of the helmet and sent the oversize headgear to Mel's Adam's apple.

Wally Ross was the park's superintendent. He ran away from a farm in Missouri with a circus. Elephants were his first love, and the trainer caught him watching practice through a knothole. He was chastised with a hickory cane. The next day he was back, and caught again, but to his surprise the trainer told him, "If you want to learn this bad, no one can prevent you from it." And took him on as his assistant.

Chief Henry Tindall was a full-blooded Navajo. He grew up on a reservation. With the chief it was hard to tell fact from fiction. His expression, like a cigar-store Indian's, never changed. One day he came home from a visit to some distant relatives and the family welcomed him with a feast. After dinner he asked about his favorite mutt, Scruffy, and when his whistles went unanswered, he asked his grandmother, "What do you think you just ate?" asked the old princess.

At the other end of the spectrum, Henry's face could be as expressive as Marcel Marceau's. He was a chimp and orangutan specialist, and when he imitated his charges, he turned into an ape. He was quite well off and had no chip on his shoulder but refused to celebrate the Fourth of July. "Why should I celebrate? It's not an Indian holiday. I was here first."

Two officers came from the Air Force to take Buster, a huge old chimp, one of Henry's retired pets. Tranquilization was the only way to move him, but he knew something was fishy and knocked the flying syringe out of the air. Henry stood by with his toniest expression. Finally, one of the officers got Buster's attention with a can of beer while the other hit him in the butt with a dart. As the ape was getting groggy, Henry finally spoke, "I told you Buster, never trust a white man."

Chief Henry, I hope you got yourself a full-blooded Navajo angel to guide you on the happy hunting grounds.

The most famous character at Jungleland was Mabel Stark, the first woman to take on a group of tigers. No one knew her exact age, but she was in her eighties when I met her. Her round face and piercing eyes resembled an old tigress except that she was tougher than any of her charges. After World War II, a young man, Pat Anthony, came to Jungleland to learn lion taming on the G.I. Bill. Yes, you could do that then. For three weeks this ambitious youngster watched Mabel put her cats through their paces. Then he made a big mistake. He walked up to her and said, "Mabel, I watched you now long enough. I think I learned all I can. Why don't you retire, and I'll take over your act." Like Mount Vesuvius, Mabel exploded, picked up a two-by-four, and chased Pat all over the grounds. "You damned whipper snapper, you'd never make cage boy if you watched me for a hundred years. In fact, you'll never be anything because I am going to kill you." Later on, Pat did become one of the finest lion trainers, but he never took over Mabel's act.

To see her tender side, you had to watch from a distance or approach silently when she talked to these beautiful cats. Slowed by arthritis, scar knitted to scar, her left arm partially paralyzed; in 1968, the insurance company refused to cover her, and she was forced to retire. She lived only a short distance away, but she never returned to visit. Who knows what her feelings were? One fact is certain. She loved her tigers more than anything in her long, colorful life. Four months later, she took a bottle of sleeping pills and tied a plastic bag around her head. Her old Cadillac was sold to pay for her funeral and the last month's rent on her small apartment. She was hard to like but easy to admire.

My first major assignment at Jungleland was on the TV series *The Green Hornet*. "Side kick" in this case was more than a figure of speech. Kato was the king of kung fu; Bruce Lee and he could kick in any direction. In the episode "Programmed for Death," the bad guy slips a tiny transmitter in the victim's pocket and turns his leopard loose to find the source and kill. We took three leopards to play the part, but Sinbad and Princess never got off the truck. Lolita was in great shape after the Disney movie and insisted on playing the part without doubles. I doubled for her victims: both the hero and the villain. With the combination of jump, knockdown, and rolling on the ground, we delivered a convincing fight scene.

At this time, Jungleland was preparing to film the biggest animal picture up until then. The story of the pudgy little veterinarian from Puddleby on the Marsh, Dr. Dolittle. The role went to six-foot-three Rex Harrison, a fine actor if not the best Dr. Dolittle, at least from a trainer's point of view. For instance, there are at least one hundred and one wrong ways to hold a bird on your hand and only one correct way. On the first day, I showed Rexy how to hold my parrot Sapphire, who played the parrot Polinesia, the wise avian teacher. Six months later, Mr. Harrison still held the bird like a contortionist. On the other hand, Anthony Newley mastered it after only one try.

I was also the assistant seal trainer and backup rider for Mary the rhino and Tall Boy the giraffe. Mary was named after the rhino that, decades ago, menaced Jane and Cheetah the chimp and dramatically expired under Tarzan's rubber knife. In our movie, she served as the jungle taxi for the good doctor. She had to be ridden. The same duty was assigned to the two giraffes, Tall Boy and Low Boy. Mary was simple. The rider wore a harness, and if she became unruly he was hoisted in the air out of harm's way.

Riding Tall Boy in Dr. Doolittle

Tall Boy wasn't fully grown yet. Only thirteen feet, but even the lankiest cowboy couldn't just mosey up to him and throw a saddle on his back. A padded stall was designed with slats cut at the right spots for saddling. He'd enter the stall and munch on oats and molasses while he got used to the touch of human hands and the weight of a saddle. He walked around the arena rider-less for a while. Then came sandbags for weight, and finally a human guinea pig had to brave the heights. This role fell to a cowboy named Dave Hall and myself. I am hardly a rider, but this I just had to try. Dave rode broncos and Brahmas, but if Tall Boy wanted him out of the saddle, the best he could do was pick his moment to fly. Once, he fell too close to the flying hoofs, and a hind leg connected with his sternum. For a while, his flight was checked and reversed as he flew a few feet up before hitting the dust.

Not being a cowboy, my technique was very simple. Hang on to the saddle horn with grim determination and pick a soft spot for a landing. Shake the dust off and try again. Wally, eight years my senior, looked at us and shook his head: "Ten years from now, you won't be this bouncy." With time, Tall Boy's acrobatics became less drastic. The exception was the first ride of the morning. He bucked and twisted until the rider bit the dust, then he was like a lamb the rest of the day. David and I used to draw for the privilege of the morning dumping. Casey Tibbs, the rodeo champion, watched one of our early sessions. We offered him a ride. He politely but firmly turned it down. The star himself rode the giraffe while he was in the harnessing chute, movements controlled. Rexy could afford to relax and wave at the monkeys in the thick jungle of the Twentieth Century Fox movie ranch, now Malibu State Park, an ideal location. A studio executive remarked, "If we could recreate the African clouds and flat-topped acacia trees, we'd never go on location."

Special effects created a thundering waterfall. Four fire hoses on a cliff, and, on "action," an instant Victoria Falls created a rainbow for the cameras. In the lake under the rainbow frolicked our hippo, Nila. She came from a show business family. Her father, Gus, starred in several jungle movies mostly in the nearby Lake Sherwood, the scene of the first Robin Hood film. Gus had a good time in the lake and refused to come out when his part was over. At night he ate all the goodies left on shore, but during daytime he just shook his stubby ears at the moving van. The studio built a trap out of steel culvert pipe with two guillotine doors. The middle was packed with lettuce and mangoes, his favorite. At midnight he visited the trap, munched on the offerings, but only the front door clanged shut. After finishing his snack, he backed out and into the lake, but from now on he wouldn't enter the trap for any goodies. He grazed on grass and weeds on the shore. He could do without his fruit salad.

Finally someone remembered the little person keeper, Half Pint, whom Gus hated more than he loved mangoes. For a large bonus, Half Pint became the bait. Gus shot out of the water like a berserk submarine. Half Pint ran into the culvert and rolled out the other end with a half second to spare, and this time both doors clanged shut as planned. Nila must have heard this story about his grouchy dad. Her scene was in the can, developed, and shown at dailies, and she still refused to come out of the lake.

Two idiots, Dave and I, dove from the cliff and swam to shore, hoping she would follow. She answered with a fetid bubble of gas from the depths. Hippos are purely vegetarian, any zoological textbook will tell us that. Nila was the exception. Jungleland had scores of Bantie chicks nesting and multiplying on the grounds. If any of them was unfortunate enough to land in her pool, the wide jaw crushed and swallowed the unlucky chicken, feathers and all. Roland, the bird trainer, had a rooster on the set made up as an exotic fantasy fowl. To sacrifice it was out of the question, but to entice Nila all he had to do was shake his pet on the shore for a squawk, and Nila was out of the pool for a feathered snack. Next, the squawk came from her trailer, and she waddled up the ramp and, with disappointment, ate the lettuce that somehow replaced the rooster.

There was an elephant scene to be shot on the same location. Wally and Tony Gentry, another seasoned elephant hand, went back to the ranch to get Bimbo and Betty, two large Asian pachyderms. The semi was two hours late, and Wally returned with Bimbo only and Tony in the hospital. If a cat attacks, most of the time it is done in a temporary rage. An elephant plans his mischief. Betty had a reputation for being tough, but she was a good worker and a beautiful specimen. With two expert trainers, no problem was expected.

The two elephants were already secured in the trucks. Wally said, "Okay, Cap, let's walk out of here." Betty reached back and grabbed Tony around the waist and methodically started to bang his head against the wall of the trailer. Wally spun around, hearing Bimbo's frightened trumpeting. She pressed so close to Betty that there was no room for Wally to get his friend out. Betty changed tactics. She dropped Tony, and with one pillar-like foot she rolled him back and forth like a housewife rolling dough. Wally now had a desperate chance to interfere. Crawling between Betty's legs, he stuck his hook in Tony's buttocks. The muscle ripped but his belt held, and he pulled his colleague free. Filming continued in a very subdued mood.

That evening, when we went to visit, Tony was unconscious. All but two of his ribs and his collarbone snapped during Betty's rolling pin exercise. His head was bandaged like a mummy's, and he had a drain installed in his thigh where the elephant's blunt molars left the muscles torn. The next day Tony was able to talk, and four weeks later he was back on the job. "You clowns don't think I'd miss a trip to the island of St. Lucia?"

The next location of *Dr. Dolittle* was on this beautiful island, an emerald gem of the British West Indies. I accompanied three chimps, three sea lions, three macaws, and three dogs on an endless cargo flight. Marigot Bay, the most picturesque spot on the island, was our headquarters. Rex Harrison and his wife, Rachel, lived on a yacht. Coming home in the evening, Don, the trainer of Gip the dog, found his suitcase on the sidewalk. Rachel had decided she needed a place on dry land as well and had Don evicted in his absence. Naturally, he objected to this rude treatment. The result: he was banned from the set, and I took over working Gip. The wife of the star has more power than a trainer.

Many of the film's scenes were shot on *Flounder*, the good Doctor's sailing ship. Captain Freddy Zendar brought the vessel from California to St. Lucia. Freddy was sixty-four years old and the horniest sailor ever to hit a port. He loved the island and its tall, coffee-and-cream-colored women. "What a paradise! Every night, a different cappuccino," he cackled in his Swiss-accented English. Among the trainers, I was the only one to bring a good supply of Johnnies, as the Brits call prophylactics. I was the rubber baron of the island, issuing the goodies on request. I know that Uncle Freddy wasn't just talking. If he did not have female company every night, he would get a terrible headache.

The four weeks spent on this lovely island went fast, and we were back in California before Christmas. During our absence, a second accident happened at the park. Jayne Mansfield and her son, Zoltan, came to visit and pose for publicity shots. The child was in the care of her psychiatrist but somehow wandered away and walked up to a young lion on a chain. He stood on the animal's paws and tried to pet it. With our absence, the place was short of trainers, and Jayne probably distracted those on duty. The results were predictable. The lion grabbed Zoltan and held his head between his paws. A second later, the trainer nearby dove on the lion, pried his jaws loose, and freed the boy. His injuries were not serious, but an infection kept him in the hospital for a while. As far as I know, he fully recovered. Accidents to other people are the nightmare of all trainers. If we get chewed up it is unpleasant, but to get someone hurt is a sheer horror.

By March 1967, *Dr. Dolittle* was in the can. I felt rich with my studio earnings and bought my first new car, a black and red Camaro. My next investment was a piece of land twenty minutes from town. It was wild California bush land, no electricity or phone lines, but since the Russians liberated our farm in 1945, it was the first piece of land I could call my own. I still had some cash left and took a six-week vacation to see Africa. While in the air, the headline of the *Herald-Tribune* glared at me. "Jayne Mansfield and her lawyer killed in a car accident. Her son, riding in the back seat, survived."

After dreaming about it for nearly three decades, I landed on African soil at Nairobi's Embakasi Airport. I had no plans, no bookings, not even a credit card, and only a handful of cash. The bearded Sikh officer asked me where I was staying. "At the Norfolk," I said confidently. I knew this establishment as the starting point for all East African safaris. The watering hole for famed white hunters, for Ernest Hemingway and for Teddy Roosevelt. Unfortunately, the Norfolk did not know about me. The lady at reception turned me down. "No bookings, no vacancy."

I found a room at the Ambassador and started to roam the streets, soaking up the sights, sounds, and smells of this fascinating city. It was three years after independence, Uhuru in Swahili. Visiting Maasai warriors in their red togas stood like storks on the street corner and jumped when a taxi blared at them. The stoic expression on their faces said, "What happened to us?" Dust-covered

Land Rovers, the indestructible beasts of burden of the bush, parked near the New Stanley Hotel. The African gun bearer guarded the vehicles, while in the Stanley's Long Bar white hunters gathered for a cool Tusker beer and to swap stories, information, and lies. I melted into the crowd and soaked up every word.

The next day I signed up with Thorn Tree Safaris. I liked their logo the best. Nowadays I would not be caught dead in a zebra-striped tourist bus, but on my first trip I had little choice. There were only three of us: a doctor from California, a young lady from Brooklyn, and myself. In this company, I was definitely the Africa "expert." We left the pavement at the village of Sultan Hammud, what a wonderful name, and entered the vast plains of Amboseli. The never seen and yet so familiar sights, the flat-top acacias, the turreted castles of termite hills, even the red dust of the road said welcome.

That night, after the other guests retired, I couldn't leave the dying embers of the campfire. The eerie wail of the hyenas, the staccato bark of the zebra stallion, the distant thunder of a lion's roar, kept me riveted to my log seat. I remembered the first time I heard the king raise his voice at the Budapest zoo and my awed remark, "I don't think we'll have enough money to send me to shoot lions." The night watchman kept an eye on me from the dark shadows of a thorn tree. Just another crazy muzungu, white man, he must have thought. Around midnight, the clouds lifted from the snowy peak of Kilimanjaro: an icy arc above the plains. A mystic domain where ghosts of ancient warriors and phantom elephants roam. The diamonds of the Southern Cross started to fade on the black velvet sky when I finally turned in. Let's leave some wonders for tomorrow.

In Arusha, Tanzania, we spent the night at the Mt. Meru Game Sanctuary. The owner, Andreas von Nagy, was one of the many I bombarded with letters seeking employment in1957 when I was a refugee in Vienna. Very reasonably, his polite answer was, "Try to learn a decent trade, kid." I told his daughter, Diana, that I'd like to see her father. He had just returned from a long day on Mt. Meru but still came to see me. When I explained who I was, his reluctance and fatigue disappeared, and I was invited to stay at his place. "I'll show you the Africa the tourists don't see." The next morning, the zebra-striped bus left without me, and I roamed the plains and mountains with my host and, now, friend for life.

Just a few chapters of Andreas' life would make Indiana Jones blush with envy. He was an officer in the elite Gendarmes Corps during the war, but his interest was always nature and wild game. After 1945, he became the manager of a state reserve and witnessed the suddenly developing taste of the new ruling class for the old aristocratic pastime of hunting. Mathias Rakosi, the bald-as-a-cue-ball Stalin of Hungary, was one of his shooting guests. Andreas' diplomatic manners and deep knowledge of the game must have left an impression on even this ruthless monster.

Of course, the first secretary of the Communist Party was not bound by rules of season or other restraints. He shot the forbidden hen as well as the long-tailed cock pheasant. He remarked sarcastically, "I noticed in your reserve even the pheasants are reactionary. When I fired at it, it was a cock; when it hit the ground, it was a hen." A bit of contemporary party humor. Later on, Andreas got into serious trouble. A plague hit his pheasant breeding station, and the birds started to die by the hundreds. He was arrested and charged with sabotage. The state prosecutor asked for and got the death sentence for willfully destroying the peoples' property. Only days separated him from his appointment with the hangman when the powerful little dictator Rakosi heard of his plight. "Well, I don't think we should hang him yet. Give him one more chance."

Without explanation, he was turned loose. The next night, with his four-year-old daughter and expecting wife, he set out for the Austrian border. The tension and fear of the illegal border crossing was just too much for the pregnant woman. She had a nervous breakdown from which she never recovered. Andreas worked for a while at the private zoo of the carmaker Opel, then found his way to East Africa. His home at the foot of Mt. Meru is a breathtaking spot. A large portion of the mountain is his private reserve, rented from the state of Tanzania.

When a month later I returned to Jungleland, I received an unexpected honor. Mabel Stark was having a late afternoon beer in the cafeteria when I arrived. Up to now she had ignored me, but on this occasion she actually left her chair, came up, and shook my hand.

"And did you see any lions in the wild?"

"Yes, Mabel, and they are wonderful."

After *Dr. Dolittle* wrapped, the park puttered on at a slow pace. The taxes were exorbitant, the upkeep high, and there were rumors of closing.

I got the title of talent coordinator. I organized the number and sequence of shows for the public. Not Mabel's of course. She always performed at her own set times. At 1 p.m. and 4 p.m., she entered the old steel arena, signaled her assistants, and her favorite tiger, Goldie, slunk through the tunnel followed by the rest. Whether the bleachers were crowded or empty, she worked through her routine. On a rainy day, the park was closed, but we were expecting a carload of studio executives. The film version of the book *Nine Tiger Man* was at the serious talking stage. The manager asked Mabel to delay her act if the big wigs were late. She just shrugged. At five to four still no limousine. At four on the dot, Mabel entered the show ring. She bowed to the empty seats and called for Goldie. At the end of the act, she bowed to the invisible audience once more. She gave her buggy whip to the cage boy and departed. When the executives did show up at 4:30 p.m., she was having her second beer in the cafeteria. Somehow the movie was never made.

On the main stage, we had a lion act, Chief Henry and his chimps, Wally and his elephants, a bird act, and two sea lions and two bears. I had just finished working the lion act and was on my way to the dressing room. The bears were next, and I had to pass by them as I had done many times. It was a hot Santa Ana wind day, and the bigger bear reached out and hit my forehead. In the mirror I could see the skull under the ripped skin. I heal fast. Today the scar is hardly visible.

After Mabel's tigers, the lions were the big attraction. Tarzan was the most handsome of the group. His thick black mane continued on his belly down to his loins. Simba was the smallest and the smartest. Numa and Congo were brothers and conspirators. For weeks they would work smooth as silk, then Congo would wink at Numa, "Let's get Simba." On an Easter Sunday, I had an exceptionally spectacular skirmish. The fur flew for fifteen minutes before peace was established. When I emerged from the dressing room, a little old lady came up to me and shook my hand, "Sonny, I have watched many lion acts, but this was the best . . ." She thought the donnybrook at the end was a regular part of my efforts.

It was during the lion act that I had the biggest scare of my life, but it wasn't Congo or Numa that frightened me. It was an old Clyde Beatty-style act, and a 38-special with blanks as a part of my equipment. I used it on rare occasions to break up fights. Never aim at the lion's body but to the side of the mane. The loud noise diverts attention and creates a moment for the next step. Alex borrowed my gun, and when he returned it I holstered it unchecked. Luckily, I had no need to use it during the act. Later, I checked the chambers. There were four blanks and two live rounds in the cylinder. I nearly fainted. What if I had wounded a lion? What if the bullet ricocheted and hit a stagehand? What if I wounded a member of the audience? What if . . .? The old saying is true. Most accidents are caused by empty guns.

Jungleland was one of the most unusual stations of my life. Its history of the people and the animals there touched my life.

My Lion act at Jungleland

CHAPTER 10

TO THE ISLAND OF DROON OR OTTERELY RIDICULOUS

My next overseas job took me to Scotland to film *Ring of Bright Water*, the story of an otter and an eccentric Scotsman based on the bestseller by Gavin Maxwell. On this production, the slogan was a line from the movie. Virginia McKenna is looking for the lost otter. The lonely lighthouse keeper points to a black dot on the misty horizon. "The wee thing swam to the island of Droon." The director, Jack Couffer, was a member of the Disney field producer school, and we hit it off right away. We stayed friends for the next forty years.

We took six otters to Oban, on the west coast of Scotland. Five came from a trout farm in Wisconsin. The owners of the farm, Tom and Mabel, trapped the first otter they owned, and their love affair with Lutra Canadiensis began. The sixth member of the cast, Oliver, was the pet of a dentist in Laguna Beach,

California. He had to give him up or face an expensive divorce. Oliver would just as soon dine on his wife's toes than on mackerel. During the shoot, the crew called him Fingers Oliver or, with even more respect, Mr. Fingers. Luckily, Oliver liked me and left my digits where they belong. He also taught me a lot about his slippery, mercurial, intelligent kind.

The rock base of all motion picture animal training is the A-B call. Someone releases the animal at point A. He is called to point B, and during his journey, the camera rolls. Timing is always important. When an animal is released in the open, the variety of distractions is endless. The word "ready" from the cameraman should really mean "ready" and not "just a second." Our director understood this simple but very important request of mine. Woe upon the focus puller who stretched his tape or the grip who adjusted a flag after the word "ready" had been uttered.

All movies need close-ups, especially of the stars, and otters were the main attraction of *Ring of Bright Water*. The human stars, Bill Travers and Virginia McKenna, of *Born Free* fame, obliged easily for right profile, left profile, and full faces. Oliver wasn't nearly as willing. Otters have two speeds, sleep and run. I had to find a way to slow him down and stay in the same spot for the otter equivalent of eternity: ten seconds. I invented or stumbled on something that since then has become a standard for film animals: hitting and holding a mark, like an actor stopping on a piece of tape on the floor.

Oliver in Ring of Bright Water

I started in a room that had four walls and a footstool, with a minimum excuse for distractions. Oliver got his mixture of fish, eggs, and cottage cheese when he climbed on the seat. Once he understood this, I covered the stool with a burlap bag and let him mark it with his strong, musky scent. For the next session, the chair disappeared and only the burlap folded in half remained. He ran around, looking for the elevation. When he hit the cloth, I bridged him with a sharp "Good." His eyes lit up, "Aha, we changed the game. I get my goodies on this thing now." Gradually, I cut down the burlap to the size of a silver dollar: an object this small could be hidden almost anywhere. Oliver found it and stood like a furry exclamation mark for the important close-ups and other shots. An animal that could hit the mark was created. The other basic tool of the movie trainer, and the blight of the sound man, is the buzzer. The adapted application of the Pavlovian reflex, sound associated with food.

The combination of buzzer and mark was used on the following scene. Jack explained it to me: "For our next trick, I want Oliver to run down to the pond and look for his usual breakfast of eels. Only this morning, the eels have buggered off to the island of Droon. Next, I want him to climb up out of the water, undulate up to Bill Travers, look over his left shoulder, shrug, and say, 'No eels.'" Sure C.J.

In translation, the following happened. Oliver is buzzed to the lake and dives in. Just out of frame, I drop a pebble in the water. He searches for it; it might be a piece of fish. He doesn't find anything edible, but completes the swim part of the scene. Bill Travers is now sitting on shore with the tiny, scent-covered rag near his feet. I call Ollie as soon as he hits dry land and utter the magic words, "On your mark": he hits the spot and sits up, expectantly looking at Bill. For the trickiest part, the look back, Mabel hit the buzzer. Not long enough for a call, only a beat, like "did I hear something?" Well, he looked back over his right shoulder instead of the left, and he did not say "No eels!" but after all, he is only an animal, and trainers are nearly human. The director was pleased with the action anyway.

Dusky, Mabel's favorite, loved Bill and Virginia. In shots like playing noses and toeses with the stars in bed, or romping with Johnny, Virginia's spaniel, Dusky was priceless.

Oliver's next big moment came as the terror on the train. Bill leaves the soggy canyons of London for the Scottish Highlands. His pet otter, Mij, has a valid dog license as a diving terrier. During the journey, Mij slips out of the cabin, climbs into jackets, fur coats, and handbags. To top his mischief, he climbs onto the shoulder of an English gentleman in a proper bowler hat, reading the

Financial Times. When the otter climbs further on his neck, the terrified gent pulls the emergency brake. The train and sequence come to a screeching halt. Of course, the English gent was played by a Hungarian-born American, me. No real actor was anxious to have Oliver sniff around his ear. It was one of my better on-camera appearances, and being an Anglophile, I relished the role with the bowler and brolly.

CHAPTER 11

LADIES AND GENTLEMEN, THIS IS OUR LAST PERFORMANCE

When I returned to Jungleland, I heard the sad news about Mabel Stark's suicide, and the rumors about financial problems became a reality. The park was just one step from bankruptcy in chapter eleven. In September, the final episode of the forty-five-year-old movie compound was acted out to a crowd of thousands.

If a movie based on the existence of Jungleland is ever made, and someone ought to do it, the script should start with the final sale. Professional auctioneers handled the affair. Everything came under the gavel: Betty, the killer elephant; Mabel Stark's steel arena; and the last rusty old wheelbarrow. Lists of items were mailed out to every zoo, animal park, and pet fancier in the country and as far away as Japan. In 1969, the tidal wave of permits and licenses that exists today was only a bureaucratic trickle. A hippo in the pool or a cheetah in the backyard was not unheard of. I am not condoning this attitude or behavior, but this is a part of history.

The auction had a combination of circus and country fair atmosphere. Among the buyers and curiosity seekers, there were somber faces who knew they were witnessing the final curtain of an era that shall never return. The crowd was seated in the bleachers in the main show area, and when the M.C. announced in a shaky voice, "Ladies and gentlemen, this is our last performance," for a few seconds the crowd fell silent. A somber, quiet dignity prevailed over the funeral of a part of California motion picture history.

After the final act, the feeding frenzy of the auction commenced. Buckets of rusty nails, handless hammers, sold for twice the value. A middle-aged woman bought one of Chief Henry's rejected chimps and was very surprised to hear that she could not make a house pet out of it. "Why not? I love him so much." A swimming pool contractor bought Nila, the chicken-devouring hippo. For transport, he rented a U-Haul and was on his way to Bakersfield. Somewhere in the San Joaquin Valley, Nila decided it was time for a little sightseeing. She pushed her big square nose against the aluminum side—strong, but not hippo-proof—and she plopped out onto the highway. She was harvesting lettuce in the fields when a nearby zoo with proper transportation collected her. By now, the pool dealer was happy to donate her to the Fresno Zoo. The owner of an Italian restaurant bought Betty the mangler. He learned from the pool dealer's problems with Nila and hired Wally and me to deliver her. As long as Wally was in sight, Betty behaved like a lady. I even rode on her head like an Indian mahout.

From the auction I ended up with a rickety wheelbarrow, an orange house cat named Pango-Pango (his friends could call him just Pango), Mabel's steel arena, and of course my priceless memories.

CHAPTER 12

THERE IS NO BUSINESS LIKE MONKEY BUSINESS

Jungleland was now past history, but for once I did not have to look for a job. ABC started a new series: a take-off on James Bond. Secret codes, fast cars, stun guns and stunning blondes, microfilm sewn into a banana, and not a single human in the cast. The series was called *Lance Link, Secret Chimp*. As you may have guessed, Lance Link, the bumbling hero; his sidekick and love interest, Mata Hairy; and his boss, Commander Darwin, were all chimpanzees. They worked for an agency: A.P.E., Agency to Prevent Evil. The members of the opposition belonged to C.H.U.M.P., or Criminal Headquarters of Underworld Master Planning. An orangutan played a Hitchockian character every episode. He was a hitchhiker, a patient in a dentist office, a sunbather in a polka dot suit, and his part was never explained. Just like the portly master of suspense, he flashed on screen and off.

The writer/producers of the show, Stan and Mike, both had vivid imaginations and an excellent sense of comedy. People still remember the series as one of the best efforts on TV. The escapades of Lance Link and his squeaky-voiced amorata still turn up in syndication. Up to now, my exposure to Chimps consisted of listening to Chief Henry's amazing tales. To help with my limited skill, I was given Corky, Henry's last pupil, with whom I had at least a nodding acquaintance. It was a good idea but it didn't work. Corky didn't want me as his acting coach. He wanted Wally. Wally's ape, a crusty old chimp twice Corky's age, did not care for him but for some reason liked me. As the weeks and months of work passed, I grew fond of Big Charley and vice versa.

Volumes have been written about the intelligence, social structure, and ferocity of our closest relative on the evolutionary ladder. After less than a month of observation, I could support Jane Goodall's "startling" discovery about tool using and meat eating. I can also add that chimps are the only animals that can laugh, cry, and lie to humans as well as each other. Not by words but by unmistakable vocalization and body language. A chimp begging for a cup of coffee is unmistakable, or is it?

Chuck, a tall misanthrope who hated everybody except his master, Larry, played the role of Ali Assassin. Larry was dressing Chuck in his desert robes when Wally happened by with coffee. Wally was and is one of the best all-around trainers, and he certainly knows chimp language. Chuck's behavior was so convincingly gimme-gimme that Wally got in reach and put the paper cup in the outstretched wrinkly palm of the ape. But Chuck lied. He did not want the coffee at all. He wanted to sink his fangs into the gullible human's hand. Larry did a very brave and the only correct thing one can do in a situation like this. He slammed his own hand in the chimp's mouth. When Chuck realized he was chewing on his master, he released at once.

Another favorite lie of Chuck's was used when he was tied out on a long leash. He'd collect about three feet of his tether in one hand and stretch to the very end as if he could not go an inch further. With his right hand he would beg for food or friendship. If an unsuspecting altruist offered him either, he'd drop the extra length of leash and, with a blood-curdling scream, attacked the sucker.

Big Charlie and Lance Link

I am sure an old chimp would make a better protection animal than any Doberman. I was inside the chain link run with Charley when our vet came to visit. I gave the word "attack," and Charley haired up like a hundred-pound porcupine and leaped at the fence. The good doctor did not think my prank was funny at all. I suppose not all animal trainers' jokes are funny, and I never sicked old Charley on anyone after that, even with the chain link in between. Charley was a great improviser. In the role of the photographer, he learned to push the exposure button without prompting. His main part was Kato, the villain's chauffeur. When he was called on to ride a motorcycle, he found the starter, kicked the transmission into gear, and accidentally drove through the studio gates into a back alley. It was a short ride. He rammed his bike into a garbage truck and started to rummage for food. I wonder what the driver of the truck told his wife that evening, "Honey, you're not going to believe this, but a huge hairy ape in a chauffeur's uniform dented my fender."

Corky as medicine man

We were filming a Wild West episode in the Malibu Hills. Corky was dressed as "Leaping Frog," the medicine man. He wore buckskin pantaloons, war paint, and a wig with pigtails. He also had to ride a pony, which he was quite good at, up to a slow trot, but when his mount suddenly reared, he threw the panic switch and ran off into the thick chaparral. Our search was fruitless for an hour, then he returned but not by himself. He was clutching the hand of a hippy also dressed in beads and feathers. In his left hand, he carried his wig and proudly handed it to Wally. The hippy's only comment was, "Hey man, what's your monkey been smoking? I want some of it!"

In San Diego we filmed on a Chinese junk, the lair of the oriental femme fatale "Dragon Woman," also played by Corky in a silk dress and sporting a lacquer fan. A small dinghy carried the crew from shore to boat. Corky looked fascinated at the cormorants fishing on the ocean. One of the birds dove and vanished under the water. Corky's eyes were glued to the spot and started to bark a distress call. He wanted to warn that bird about the dangers of drowning. Chimps cannot swim a lick.

Tonga, the simian James Bond, was fastidiously clean. In a pillow fight with his adversary, "Baron von Butcher," the pillow burst and a snowstorm of chicken feathers covered the set. Von Butcher kept pummeling Tonga, but as soon as a feather landed on our hero's blazer, he stopped and picked the fuzz from his neat blue jacket.

My chimp, Big Charley, had an insatiable appetite. Before the pie fight scene, I tried to fill him up, but he would have eaten the total budget for props. From whipped cream, I switched to shaving cream. "Oh goody," he said and kept devouring it. Finally, we found a strongly mentholated version, which he left alone long enough to finish the pie fight of the century.

To create a different character from the same animal, we used a whole range of human makeup, moustaches, and beards. As Baron von Butcher, Charley sported a monocle but was bare faced. As Kato, he wore a Clark Gable moustache. Anyone who has had to wear makeup knows that as the day wears on the whiskers get itchy. He used his nails to scratch, and if I did not watch him the offending hairpiece would vanish. He got very good at it. We were waiting on the set, Charley on my lap facing me, his hands in sight. Very affectionately, he put his head on my shoulder. I was touched, but when the director called "action," the moustache was gone, and I noticed a suspicious movement of his cheeks. His tongue shifted something. While he was resting his head on my shoulder, the rubbery lips removed and hid the moustache like a convict hides a smuggled-in file.

Corky and Charley played a gypsy fortune-teller routine. Charley was the oracle. To get him to pay close attention to the clients' hand, I stuck tiny bits of tape to his palm. With real concentration, he looked at Corky's hand and touched the black dots with his long index finger. On camera, it looked like the fortune-teller tracing the lifeline of his client. During filming, the long shot is followed by the medium shot and close-ups. After every take, Charley was getting less fascinated with the bits of tape trick. He hooked one with his fingernail and lifted it off Corky's palm. At my disapproving glance, he gave me the look of a little boy caught with a frog. He licked the tape like a postage stamp and stuck it back on Corky's palm. Even taped it to make sure it stuck.

The only exception to the simian cast was a robot gorilla created by the crazed scientist, "Dr. Strangemind." I played the robot. Charley was the scientist. He wore a velvet coat and a cape and added a touch to his part all on his own. When he made his entrance, he covered his face with the hem of his cape a la Bela Lugosi. My transformation into the mechanical gorilla was a bit too fast for him. Through the slits in the rubber mask I saw his expression shift from marvel to challenge, and in the next instant he jumped me. I tore off the mask while he was in midair, and instead of fight, he hugged me and made it so natural, like it was his intention all along: "Who me? I never wanted to box the gorilla's ears."

The Lance Link Band was part of every show. Corky played the violin with deep feeling, like Yehudi Menuhin, bowing and weaving to the tunes of a melody only he could hear. Tonga played a mean sax, and Taffy, the least talented of the group, was the drummer. This was her only strong point, and she made the most of it. The earliest form of music was probably apes making noise on a moonlit jungle glade, with fists and broken branches, on mounds of hard clay and hollow logs. This ancient ritual must have surfaced in Taffy. At the end of the series, we all agreed that no trainer ever worked harder or laughed harder than we on *Lance Link, Secret Chimp*.

Now that Jungleland was torn apart by progress, I decided to hang out my shingle and start my own company. My collection was small. Lolita the leopard, two dogs, Witch the falcon, Sapphire the macaw, and Algae, a sea lion. She was beached with a heavy infestation of lungworms. My vet gave her six months to live. Eighteen years later, she is still very much alive and swimming.

For my first company name, I picked Ungawa Bwana Animal Rentals. Ungawa is the magic Hollywood Swahili word in the old Tarzan movies. Johnny Weissmuller would send his elephants to destroy a hostile village or instruct Cheetah to rescue Jane from cannibals with the same phrase: *ungawa*. It was definitely an unusual name to call a business, perhaps a bit too unusual. When I handed out my card, I had too much explaining to do, and after six months I changed it to the more prosaic but self-explanatory Animal Actors of Hollywood.

On my first job as an independent, I doubled for a vampire. I took a charge from Alex's Doberman, and with the super-human strength of a bloodsucker, I cracked his back. Or so it looked. The real dog jumped me, and I broke the backbone of a realistic dummy. If you think this is unusual, I also slapped a nude woman with a buggy whip while she was riding a hog. It sounds kinkier than it was. The story was about witches, and the actress used a good-natured sow as her mount. On "action," Yolanda was to run down the hill, but she just stood there doing nothing. I was about to give her a slap with the whip, but she turned, and my slap landed across the actress' thigh. She was a good sport and did not put a hex on me.

My friend Jack, the director of *Ring of Bright Water*, was in production to do *Living Free*, the sequel to *Born Free*. I was picked to organize and train the lion department. Drive-through Safari parks in California and Florida had more cubs than they knew what to do with. Lucky for us. The story followed Jespah, Gopah, and little Elsa from infancy to their release in the Serengeti. We needed sets of three at different ages plus one double for each group. We also needed two adult lionesses to portray Elsa in the flashbacks. When our plane arrived in Nairobi, we had fifteen lions waiting for the government vet's inspection. I have heard the question a million times: "Coals to Newcastle, lions to Africa?" The answer is simple. Even if I were allowed to catch lions on the Serengeti, they would not react to the director's wishes, at least not in a satisfactory manner.

From the animal trainer's perspective *Living Free* was a difficult movie to make. In just about every take, I had to have three rambunctious cubs doing specific things. The script called for a wide scale of moods from sad to hilarious. All three had to travel at the same speed and refrain from grab-assing, the favorite behavior of all young animals, especially pint-sized lions. Jack was concerned about losing our actors in the bush. Based on my experience with Sabor, I was not concerned with that. Lions are not easy to lose.

"Campi ya Simba" or Lion Camp was located on the shores of Lake Naivasha in the Great Rift Valley about an hour's drive from Nairobi. The compound was nestled under the shade of yellow-barked fever trees. Our civilized, jet-lagged lions surveyed the landscape of their ancestors. The first thing they had to learn about Africa: the vegetation is equipped with thorns. Creepers with yellow flowers, the umbrella-shaped acacias, the stunted whistling thorn, all bristled with nature's switchblades. Walks on the innocent looking shore ended up with a sticker in the soft paws. At first the cubs stopped with a paw raised like a birddog on point, looking at us for help, but they soon learned to pull the offending sticker out with their sharp baby teeth.

Assistance with the training and care of the cubs was provided by Cheryl, the youngest trainer at the former Jungleland, and Marques a Bisletti, a Kenyan resident who raised lions long before Joy Adamson's attempt. As a result, Joy hated her. A half-moon shaped island on the rim of an extinct volcano was ideal for training and filming.

The best group of cubs was named Ace, Mace, and Hairless Joe, who was named after a character in the comic strip "Li'l Abner." A day after naming them, I noticed that "he" should have been called Josephine. Even after the mistake, she was called Joe throughout the picture. In the book and in the films, the cubs lose their mother at an early age and have to cope with the hardships of the bush: "It's a jungle out there, Jane!"

The orphans take over the remains of a cheetah kill just to be chased off by a mob of marabou storks, tall scavengers with beaks like a log splitting wedge. Mace, the bravest of the group, took the menace seriously and took off for the protection of the thicket. Hairless Joe stood her ground. Poachers lurk everywhere, and the cubs nearly miss getting skewered by a deadly spear trap hidden among the branches. For bait, there is a leg of lamb on the trail, but the cubs are suspicious, says the script, and approach carefully. The director insisted, as he had to, for realistic movement to make the action convincing.

I couldn't use the sound of a buzzer for a call. The approach would have been too fast. Instead, we walked the little actors down the path and praised them when they reached the desired spot. I also had to add a look up the tree to notice the spear hidden in the branches. This weapon came crashing down and sliced through the lamb shank in a separate shot. For the panic exit of the cubs, I used a buzzer, and the fast pace and direction change worked fine. Next time *Living Free* is on TV, watch closely. This thirty-second scene took us six hours to film and was well worth it.

The author, Joy Adamson, lived a short distance from our compound. Too short. She came to visit our lions, and to my surprise even the tamest, Ace, wanted to bite her. There was something in her approach that irritated all of our cats. Perhaps it was over-dedication. A barren woman's obsession with a child substitute. An attitude of "I am going to love you, maul you, pet you, whether you want me to or not." How she survived with the original Elsa is a mystery to me. I met George Adamson on a few occasions. He was a quiet old gentleman, quite deaf, and spent most of his time in the bush away from Joy. Our local contact, Johnny Bax, knew him well and, around the campfire, told us curious episodes from the life of this colorful recluse.

They were motoring along somewhere in the northern frontier of Kenya when Johnny noticed a rhino gaining on their Land Rover. He shouted at George, but not loudly enough, "Hey, George, step on it. There's an angry rhino behind us!" The Land Rover is not a silent vehicle; it is not easy to understand even with perfect hearing.

"What did you say?" said the aging game warden as he jammed on the brakes. Even George heard the loud bang as the rhino punctured the spare tire on the back door.

George's deafness was not entirely a handicap. If he got an unwanted call from Joy, he pretended not to hear a thing. "Who is that? Is that you, Joy? I can barely hear you. There is a big storm coming in from Lake Rudolph. Why don't you try back in an hour?" He'd slam down the receiver, sling his rifle over his sun-baked shoulder, and disappear into his real home, the bush.

George collected not only lions but horses as well. Little plastic white horses from his favorite whisky bottle. Joy did not approve of his modest-to-medium drinking habit. His friends knew about George's accumulated equines and saved specimens from their own empty bottles. He hung the small trophies on a string around his tent, and every time he added a new body he murmured with satisfaction, "Well, this will annoy her even more." On the rare occasion he came to Naivasha, he never stayed in the main house. He slept in a small shack at the end of the garden.

At the beginning of filming, Joy invited Cheryl and me to dinner. To my surprise, the living room furniture was covered in lion skins. I had the naughty urge to pet one and ask, "Joy, was this one Elsa?" During the first five minutes of dinner, she told me that, in Vienna, she had a Hungarian lover. "A real hot-blooded one, not like this cold fish at the end of the table." And she pointed at George who, in answer, blew a huge cloud of smoke from his pipe.

The actors of *Living Free*, Susan Hampshire and Nigel Davenport, were wonderful people. Terrified of the lions at first, and why should they not be, I soon gained their confidence. If there was any residue of doubt, it never showed on film, even when Susan had to share a camp bed with Arusha, one of the adult lionesses. I like to raise my movie animals from infancy. There's no substitute for learning about the characteristics, whims, and mood changes. Arusha was an exception. She was raised at a park in Florida, and I estimated her age at two and a half years. A young adult in her prime. She arrived later than the cubs, and even in her shipping crate her eyes told me, "We'll get along just fine."

Susan Hampshire in Living Free

Walking lions on a leash is the most difficult but necessary part of movie training. It also takes a lot of trust between man and animal. As the saying goes, "It is very hard to push on a chain." I have met circus trainers who worked a mixed group of lions and tigers, an explosive combination of nitro and dynamite, but they would not consider leading a big cat on a leash. A week after her arrival, Arusha could safely be taken anywhere on a six-foot chain. I was walking her to location past a herd of cattle. She crouched down like a kitten before a mouse hole, and her eyes flashed "dinner." At the first "no" and a slight pull on the chain, she changed her mind and walked by the unsuspecting bovines. One sequence called for a rhino to chase Elsa's cubs, who escape by climbing a tree. This was impossible to film in the wild so we had to stage it.

A sturdy log corral was built, bolted, and wired together. Carr Hartley, the best-known trapper in East Africa, supplied us with a freshly caught rhino. Once in captivity, these short-tempered pachyderms quiet down in a matter of days. Ours was caught Monday, and on Tuesday the cameras rolled. He had plenty of fire, but none of it directed toward the agile lion cubs, who could get out of his way with mocking ease. At any rate, the cubs hardly interested the rhino. His anger was directed at humans, and who could blame him?

The camera was set up safely outside the log fence. Volunteers were needed to draw the pachyderm's charge in the right direction. Our location manager, Johnny Baxondale, and I volunteered. The shortsighted animal waited till we got within his striking distance, about fifty feet. Then he lowered his colossal head, gave a whistle like an overheated team engine, and charged. Johnny and I ran toward the fence and safety. This system worked once, twice, three times, but the director wanted "just one more."

Johnny and I were getting tired. Reaching the fence, Johnny slipped, and, like a suit drying on the line, his six-foot-three body hung half in, half out. He had enough sense to stay frozen. The motion-activated prehistoric beast stopped six feet from his goal. Jumping and shouting, I drew his attention to me, and he came at double speed. As I ran, a field mouse nest collapsed under my feet. Without looking back, I jumped up, ran, and dove to safety. When I hit the ground on the outside, the rhino's horn hit the fence on the inside. According to eye witnesses, there were fifteen inches between my shorts and the avenging horns. Close enough.

CHAPTER 13

KWA-HERI MEANS "SO LONG"

In March 1974, *Born Free: The Story of Elsa the Lioness* became a TV series with Garry Collins and Diana Muldaur playing the roles of George and Joy Adamson. From *Living Free*, I had two lionesses, Arusha and her daughter, Asali, perfect for the role of Elsa. From Las Vegas, I collected a good-natured but not very bright lioness, Lamu, and a half-grown cub named Whoosie. If the series goes for more than one season, she'll grow into the part. I also needed two adult males. Near San Francisco, I found a handsome black-mane named Hatari, meaning "danger" in Swahili. Later on, he deserved his name, but at present he looked mild-mannered for a lion who had not been handled in three years.

I needed one more male, one I could use in attack scenes. Circus Vargas had one called Blake. He was a veteran movie lion once owned by Ivan Tors and a regular on *Daktari, Cowboy in Africa*, etc. Blake was eight years old and held the record for putting more holes in more trainers than any lion in motion picture history. No lost limbs or digits, but if he found an opening, he took it, and the human hide rips easily.

Blake had to be walked like a dog, heeling properly, his head just a bit ahead of the person's leg. If you relaxed and let him fall behind, he'd pinch your butt or worse. He also had the coldest eyes of any lion I ever met. Most lions have an honest look. It says "I like you" or "tolerate you" or "watch out, you are not simpatico." Expressions to read and interpret. Blake's eyes did not say anything. He looked through you like a plate of glass, but with caution he could be used in staged attacks. At least he did not have the record of Wallace the lion. I met Wallace, or rather his stuffed head, at the Circus Museum in Florida. He killed three trainers in one afternoon.

For my number one assistant, I took Cheryl. Lady trainers are by far more dedicated and more talented than men. Any of my colleagues who dispute this, let them write their own memoirs. Of course, there are occasions when men are needed, because of our usually greater muscle capacity. If the garbage gets too heavy, we can lift it easier. One more reason to have a male assistant is a male lion. The extra weight and strength makes a difference when you hold four to five hundred pounds on a chain.

I got excellent backup in Frederico. He grew up in Italy, and during the war he used to annoy the Nazi motorcycle messengers by stretching a steel cable about neck high on their route. In America, he tried being a mechanic, a used car dealer, cannabis grower, and real estate agent, among other things. In the '60s, he worked for an animal phony who tried to make a living in the movies but failed. He could not even feed his own animals, much less Fred. In the end, the phony was shot by an irate rancher for cattle rustling. The rancher, in true "Western" style, was acquitted. Fred got tired of living on monkey chow and dog food and got a job at Jungleland. He developed a fondness and talent for bears and, at the auction, ended up with two black bears, one of which cut my head open.

I figured if he could handle Nazis, he could back me up with Blake and Hatari. Besides his physical strength, Fred had other qualities useful on long-term location jobs. He did not mind if a cordon bleu chef did not cook the food or if his tent sprang a small Niagara Falls during a tropical rainstorm. In short, he was not a complainer, was a good storyteller, and had an inexhaustible supply of jokes.

One of his stories was about his former boss, the animal phony, and his jaguar named Pasha. The job was a still photograph of the jaguar leaping from A to B. The camera clicks while the jaguar is in midair. The phony took a shortcut. Instead of teaching Pasha to leap on cue, he knew that jaguars hated cougars, so he rented a stuffed specimen from a prop house, where he was told to avoid damaging the cougar at all costs. Fred's duty was to tease the jaguar to the landing platform. "But remember," Phony lectured him, "do not let Pasha get a hold of the cougar. I must return it without a hair missing."

According to the plan, Phony was going to nab the jaguar with his lasso just as he landed on the platform, thus giving Fred a chance to get the hated but valuable animal out of Pasha's reach and sight. On the word "ready," Fred shows the cougar to Pasha; his eyes get big as saucers, and he jumps with murder on his mind. Phony missed with the lasso. Fred had two choices: offer himself or sacrifice the stuffed cougar. Wisely, he did the latter and yelled, "Here Pasha, if you want it, it's yours. Props, bring the next cougar."

We arrived with the lions and Lolita, my leopard, at the end of March 1974 during the worst drought of the decade. Once we left Nairobi, cadavers of game and cattle littered the roadside. The few kongoni that loitered about at the national park were skin and bones. Only the zebras looked well fed, or their black and white stripes create an illusion of roundness. Anyway, I have never seen a skinny zebra. On April 1st the rains started, and as if touched by a magician's wand, nature revived itself. Even the skeletons of dead animals became new life with such rapidity they appeared to crawl out of sight as if ashamed of their sorry condition among this orgy of rebirth. The lions in their runs refused to take shelter from the warm tropical rain. Hatari would lie on the roof of his house like a big, hairy Snoopy. When his mane became saturated, he'd stand up and shake it, creating a halo of diamond raindrops. First unit directors changed every episode, but the second unit had a permanent leader, Jack, the director of *Ring of Bright Water*.

Filming a television series is a high-pressure task. There is only so much money and time to finish each episode, the luxury of falling behind schedule does not exist. Quite often, the animals were needed on both units. I needed at least one more assistant. I found one unexpectedly on the roadside. Just off the track in the bush, there was a man in his early twenties holding on to the tail of a snake. The reluctant head and the rest of the body were trying to disappear in a hole under the bush. It looked like a tug of war with a shiny black rope and the opposing party underground.

To my "What are you doing?" the lad answered calmly, "I am trying to catch a snake."

"What kind is it?"

"Well, it is too soon to tell. Either it is a mole snake or a spitting cobra. I won't know until I see the head."

"Won't that be too late?"

"Not really," he replied with a British Kenya accent. "I have been catching the buggers for years. My name is Richard, and the owner of the farm you are staying on is my dad. Well, not really my dad, but he will be as soon as he marries my mom, Marge. You must know her; she is the caterer."

It was my turn to surprise him. "Would you like to work with lions?"

"No, thank you. I was raised in these parts, and I know lions eat people; I'd much rather work with cobras."

That evening I met Richard again at the Lodge's bar, the headquarters of the production company and the watering hole of the local characters. I learned more about his life. He was born in England but raised in Africa by Mom and a succession of step-daddies. The one about to wed Marge would be number four.

"I make a point to attend Mother's weddings whenever I can," he remarked as a matter of fact.

The last two years he had spent in the Rhodesian Army as a trooper in the famed Selous Scouts. With a shy smile he added, "Up to this point, I have killed more people than I have f-cked." Since then, Richard has more than made up for this discrepancy.

He still did not want to become a lion tamer, but his vivacious mother, Marge, kept after me. "Give my boy a job! He'll learn fast, I am sure." She also kept clipping away at her son's resistance.

I took a weekend trip to see Andrew at his hideaway in Tanzania. The short visit was very pleasant, but I seemed to be cursed at the borders. This time it was an army checkpoint long after the border that "liberated" my Swiss Army knife. The leader of the platoon also wanted my boots, but I resisted successfully. On the way back, I met Richard on the road. I flagged him down and told him to report to work on Monday morning. He had a job. "But, but, but," he stammered a bit, but on Monday he showed up.

Whoosie, the year-old lioness, was our confidence builder with the actors and members of the crew that had to work in close proximity to the cats. She was a good size for her age but tolerant of strangers and as tame as a lion can be. I sent Richard with Cheryl and Whoosie on a get-acquainted walk through the woods. Cheryl explained the basic behavior around lions. Move slowly, and do not run should a cat come at you. It would be futile to try to outrun them. They are much faster. She also explained our hand-feeding technique, as payment for the completion of a command. Even obeying a "come here" got a reward from a flat palm, similar to giving a horse a sugar cube. She also told Richard about the use of the word "no," said in a strong firm tone, mostly as a prevention before the lion did something objectionable like grabbing a water hose or looking at a person with more than normal interest.

She did not describe the lions' way of greeting us, as our cats considered us, to a certain extent, to be part of their pride. For a while they walked side-by-side, then Cheryl handed the leash over to her student: "Here. You try it." Whoosie, quite normally, walks up to this new tall pride member and rubs up against his legs, her way of saying "Glad to meet you." All Richard could think of was "lions eat people" and bellowed a stentorian "NO!" The cub jumped six feet in the air and took off at full speed. To his credit, Richard did not drop the leash, or perhaps his fingers were frozen to it. When both slowed down, the cub crouched down at the end of the chain with her wide eyes asking, "What have I done to deserve this horrible reprimand?" Cheryl caught up with them and explained about the lion's greeting and the more subtle use of the word "no." The rest of the lesson went smoothly with some amount of trust and mutual understanding built up by the end of the day.

The next day was a bit more complicated; in fact, our trainer apprentice wished his mom had never asked me to hire him, or if she did, he would have turned the job down flatly. It was a day we'll all remember. The script called for two man-eaters, a lion and a lioness, breaking into a Maasai settlement. A group of village mongrels raise the alarm and alert the warriors. The village was an authentic replica built on Crescent Island on Lake Naivasha. The fence around the huts, according to my instructions, had weak points and branches without thorns where we could film the marauders breaking in. This was an isolated shot. Blake and Asali called to a reward, wormed through the "impenetrable" wall. Next came the confrontation between the curs and the two lions.

We hired the dogs from the shanty-town of Karakata. They were a lot harder to handle than our lions. African dogs are not pampered. They survive by their wits and scraps, wherever they can find them. For this scene, we picked the meanest looking of the lot. Inside the thorn fence were the low mud-and-cow-dung huts, replicas of original Maasai dwellings. A person of average height could enter if bent in half. Jack set up his camera, protected by a safety man equipped with a CO_2 fire extinguisher. This instrument makes a loud whooshing sound and spews out a cloud of white fume. Should the occasion arise, a blast from it is enough to change a lion's mind.

Now I replaced Blake with Hatari as I did not want to mix my wrestling cat with a lioness. A lion and a lioness in the same shot can develop into a tricky situation. If she comes into heat, which can happen at the drop of a chastity belt, he gets possessive and unworkable. At times only her presence can turn a lion into an uncontrollable raging fury. I figured if I have to do this scene, I might as well use Hatari, who was not a wrestling cat.

The lions entered first. The village mutts rushed them, bristling, barking, and growling. Hatari stood his ground, trying to figure out what got into this fresh bunch of curs. Are they trying to commit suicide or what? Asali, the huntress, reacted differently. She lunged at the noisy mob. Most of the dogs turned and ran. Two broke through the fence and hightailed it in the direction of the village. We never saw them again. The toughest stood his ground and stared down the lioness; the fourth crawled into a hut. The director yelled for at least two dogs.

Fred and I could not leave the scene, so I yelled at Richard to bring the dog out of the hut.

"Who, me?"

"Yes, of course you."

"How?"

"Any way you like, just get that dog back into the shot."

He folded his tall body in two and disappeared in the dark interior of the cow-dung shack. On the outside, the mongrel was still defying the two lions. Asali made another lunge at him, and Hatari did something totally unexpected and unexplainable. He knocked her against the side of the flimsy hut and started to roar. Lucky for us, Jack is an excellent cameraman and he got every bit of the frantic action on film and in perfect focus. It was not exactly what the writer dreamed up in Burbank, but it was a lot more, and Jack wisely decided he had enough for the script.

In the commotion, we forgot about Richard deep in the hut trying to persuade the reluctant mongrel to surface. During Hatari's outburst, the poor lad was certain the entire contraption would come down on his head, lions and all. For the sound effects, the clay walls magnified Hatari's roar like a giant base fiddle. As a last thought, Richard cursed his well-meaning mom for getting him this stupid job. The Rhodesian army was a retirement community compared to lion taming.

A tough day was followed by a pleasant evening. Two Kenyan lassies joined the production as secretaries. Margo was a tall, well-built brunette, and her friend, Heather, had an interesting face and the green eyes of a leopard speckled with gold. There are tits-and-ass men and everything in between, but a beautiful head of hair gets my attention. And this girl's hair . . . well, a cascade of gold to make Rapunzel pale with envy. A shining tangle of silk to wind around a man's heart. She sat on the couch with her legs tucked under her and looked at me with total indifference and the unintentional cruelty of youth. She was nineteen going on twenty, and I would face forty in three months. Fred seemed to be just fine with the brunette.

The next day, we continued with the "Man-eaters of Merti" episode. It was my day to get killed. I was made up like a Maasai el'moran, warrior, covered with a thick coat of red ochre and a red cloak tied over one shoulder, very much like a Roman toga. Blake was usually easy to get into a wrestling mood, but this morning it took him a while. The Maasai get-up could have put him off. I had noticed on my previous movie, *Living Free*, the strange behavior to the traditionally dressed Maasai.

Charles, the camera assistant, was a full-blooded Maasai in modern clothes, and the lions did not care, but the costume on a real or fake Maasai turned our born-in-the-U.S.A. lions inside out. It was like a reaction to being cornered by an enemy. The Maasai have been hunting lions for centuries, in defense of their cattle but also as a coming-of-age ritual. An el'moran was not considered a full-fledged warrior until he washed his spear in lion's blood. Everybody has a theory as to why our lions, whose grandparents had never seen a Maasai, would behave this way. My theory is that the silhouette triggers this violent reaction.

Whatever the reason, Blake was not in the right frame of mind to attack this morning. Finally, I turned my back on him, and he came on like a freight train and knocked me down. I let him have my left arm, and he was surprisingly gentle, just a firm hold, which I hoped would look good for the camera. After two takes from different angles, he really got into the spirit. As I was rolling under him, trying to get out, I felt his body stiffen. His front legs held my shoulder in a tight grip, and he put most of his weight on my upper half. I looked at his facial expression. Those glacial eyes did not tell me much, but his grip got tighter every second, like a dog protecting his bone. My attempts to get out from under him were in vain.

It was time for the back-up man to interfere. "Fred, take him off of me." Without a second's hesitation, he was at my side. One of the safety devices I had was a small bottle of ammonia wrapped in a rag and tied to the end of a hickory cane. When the situation calls for it, one crack and the bottle is broken, and the rag soaks up the pungent liquid. The fumes will make the animal release whatever it holds without a fight. One of the little tricks I learned from Melvin Koontz, the paragon of all movie trainers. I felt Blake's paws loosen their grip on my chest, and he moved his center of gravity off of my chest. I rolled out from under and asked Jack if he had enough footage because I certainly did for the day.

Wrestling Blake

But as the supreme reward for my efforts, I got at least a glance from Heather as I walked by the office in my Maasai warrior's finery. In the evening around the campfire, we chatted with the secretaries, finding out more about their life stories. These two were practically inseparable. Their last boyfriends were Italian, and the romance had just ended and not with the best of feelings. Heather warned Fred to take it easy and slow if he wanted Margo's trust. She was still tender from the treatment of the treacherous Dago, Her words.

Nobody gave me advice on how to approach the object of my desire, the girl with the golden mane of a lion. I had to make my own plans. There are two kinds of men: handsome and patient. I belong to the latter group. I hoped time and the location were on my side. Meanwhile, I hated the picture of the lad with the toothpaste ad smile on her desk. Every time I'd stop by to chat, she'd readjust it just in case I had failed to notice it. The more she handled the damn photo, the more I ignored it. "Who me? Jealous? Never."

For the final clinching shot of the "Man-Eater" episode, Jack wanted a shot where the lion drags the victim through the thorn fence and out of the village. A scene like this is normally done with a life-size dummy dressed appropriately and garnished with a chunk of meat. The lion grabs the bait and drags dummy and all to a quiet spot to eat. The problem is even the best artificial body looks like what it is, a lifeless dummy. After my successful wrestling with Blake, I felt I could improve on this and do a live drag, but I did not want to do the take more than once. Jack promised he would get it on the first run. The author, Joy Adamson herself, showed up to watch this attempt. Under the flimsy Maasai outfit, I had one protecting garment: a vest made of heavy leather reaching to my hips. It would give me some protection from being dragged on the ground.

Under the lion's mane, I had a short piece of chain. On the off-camera side I hooked my arm into this chain. The right arm held at the proper angle would make it look like he was dragging me by the shoulder. Fred called Blake, and to give him additional speed, Cheryl fired a short blast on the CO_2. Blake takes off, and I hang on to the chain and even manage to push my right arm in his mouth. He smashes through the barricade, gets his reward from Fred, and cut.

"Jack, did you get it?"

"Yes, but we have to repeat it."

Joy asked in her heavily Austrian-accented English (she talked quite a bit like Zsa Zsa Gabor), "But why, dahlink? It looked vonderful."

"That is true, but as you were thrashing around with the lion, I caught a glimpse of your BVDs."

Maasai wear under their shuka exactly the same as Scotsmen wear under their kilt. Nothing. Reality or not, I was going to wear something around my tender parts. I soaked my Fruit of the Loom in thick red ochre and put them on while still wet. During a stunt like this, thinking is not a good idea. Just do it, and let's get it over with. Take two, all set, but Blake is anticipating and rearing to go. It took all my strength to hang on to the chain under his mane. This time I could not give him my right arm, but the angle of the shoulder was still convincing. He breaks through the fence even faster, I let go of the chain, and Fred collects him.

Jack is pleased. "Okay, boys, that was fine; we got it in the can."

On my leather vest, just above my kidney, there was a hole torn by a branch. Lucky I wore that vest. Mrs. Adamson is all smiles and shakes my red-ochred hand.

"Dahlink, it took a crazy Hunkarian to do a stunt like this. Once, in Austria, I had a Hunkarian boyfriend, you know."

"Thank you, Joy, but that must have been a long time ago," I thought.

She had a reputation for being a man-eater herself in her younger years. She came to Africa to paint wildflowers with her Swiss husband, and George Adamson was their guide. The husband liked to wander around on his own to collect giant lobelia and such. One day he returned early and found his wife and their guide in flagrante delicto. George was terribly upset and tried to apologize, but the husband not only understood, he was downright generous. "These things happen; all I ask is that you marry her." George, obliging, did just that. I heard this story from so many people, I am convinced this is essentially what happened. In later years they grew apart, but a bond, perhaps from the early days of their relationship, remained, and when she was murdered in 1980, George cried for hours. This I also heard from a witness, I believe. There's nothing more complicated than a relationship between a man and a woman.

Speaking of such, I gave up all hope with the blonde secretary. It wasn't anything she said or did; it was what I saw. I got a glimpse of myself in the convex mirror of my Land Rover. A rear view mirror couldn't be flattering to Cary Grant, but what I saw was discouraging. Beady eyes staring from deep sockets, scraggly hair thin enough to read through, and the whole vision dominated by a prominent ethnic nose. At that instant, I gave up all thoughts about conquering the girl with the lion's mane. Let her carry a torch as big as Miss Liberty's for her Italian Adonis, but her hair and that intriguing body under that exotic kanga wouldn't leave my mind.

Over the weekend, there was a disco at the lodge. Fred, who was part gypsy and as such knew something about love potions, baked a batch of Alice B. Toklas brownies. The girls assisted him, giggly with anticipation. At ten o'clock that evening, it was two very mellow and pliant secretaries we led around the dance floor. The golden head rested on my shoulder like a sleepy kitten. That night, I did not have to watch her glide across the lawn in her long dress like a fleeting nocturnal moth. She spent the night in my bungalow, praise be to Alice B. Toklas. In the sobering light of the morning, her mood changed and everything was my fault. The only encouraging sign: the picture of the grinning Italian on the shiny motorcycle had disappeared. I was now even more patient. I knew it was worth it. Fred and Margo were happy as newlyweds, and he was even older than I and completely bald.

The scripts kept coming, some good, most of them bad, but they kept the animal department busy. Jack needed a scene of Elsa meeting elephants. We packed up and moved to the Northern Frontier with Asali riding in the back of the Land Rover. At a petrol station, the local population swarmed around our lions like metal filings drawn to a strong magnet. Ninety percent of Africans grow up without ever seeing a lion or an elephant, unlike children in Europe and America. In East Africa, there are no zoos, and a trip to a national park is not within the reach of most people.

Once in the reserve, we started looking for a single elephant. We came along a young cow in a sand river feeding on the sparse vegetation. Jack is the only cameraman who sets up his machine before I can get the animal into position. He was looking through the lens before I got Asali out. She watched the big gray thing from the bank. The wind had changed, and her trunk came up sniffing. From a low angle, it looked like a black telescope searching for a target above the riverbank.

Whether it was the lion's smell or the humans, she decided to scare us away. The agility and speed of an elephant is always surprising. The bank before us was steep, but she was out of the riverbed, scaled the steep incline, and came on trumpeting. Asali, Fred, and I ran for the only safe place available, the open back of the Land Rover. The lioness beat us all, but we were not far behind and dove in headfirst. Most of the time, an elephant's loud display is a mock charge, as this turned out to be. She put on the brakes ten feet from the radiator, gave one more loud scream, and went back to her uninterrupted grazing.

Lamu, the lioness with the lovely blonde coat but not much brain, was our next performer. She rode in Fred's truck. He maneuvered behind a bull elephant and turned her loose. The "dumb blonde" did not have Asali's reserve. Instead of a cautious approach, she rushed at the old patriarch at full speed. What was on her mind only she knew. Even a ding-a-ling like her couldn't hope to catch something that big. I don't think she thought at all, just rushed in, and the surprised elephant took off for the bush. The blonde right on his heels, like a yelping dog chasing a semi-truck. She followed him all the way into the thicket. Like the previous episode, Jack got everything on film. Deep in the vegetation, the elephant gained his composure. "Who is this pest chasing me anyway? I'll show her who the real king of the forest is."

We heard the loud clarion of the angry bull, and Lamu came out a lot faster than she entered and was glad to find me. I put her up in my vehicle. The elephant stopped at the edge, pawed the ground a few times, then went on his way. Fred drove on the other side of the grove, heard the commotion, but did not know that I had collected the dumb blonde. He saw a lion under a bush and thought it was Lamu. He got out of his car to collect her. The leash in one hand, a piece of meat in the other, he calls the lion.

"Come here, Lamu."

No reaction at all. Fred gets closer, and the lion gets up and retreats into thick cover. Now Fred was getting mad.

"Come here, Lamu, you dumb blonde bitch. It is just like you to play games with me."

He cuts the track of the moving cat and calls once more. The lion gets stiff shouldered, the tufted tail lashes its side, and he snarls at Fred. Now he suspected something was wrong and stood still. For a few seconds, it was an African standoff, then the lion turned and melted into the bush. From this angle,

Fred noticed the sprouting mane on his back. He tried to collect a wild young male instead of the dumb blonde. The episode could have had a tragic end, but it did not. The studio's publicity department loved the story, and two weeks later a London rag had Fred pick up a well-known man-eater of the Northern Frontier.

The African Cape buffalo is number one on the list of animals most feared by professional hunters. There is an unwritten rule in animal training with tame or wild animals: as soon as the camera is pointed at you, turn your ass toward it. For our next caper, we worked out a plan to avoid this with our next subject: a large herd of Cape buffalo.

Our tracker, Kipsige, reported a good size congregation moving across a dry lake bed, approaching the savannah. Jack set up his camera under a stunted tree. Kipsige stood behind him with a double-barreled Holland and Holland. This was the only occasion in six months of filming that we were backed up by fire-power. I stood on the right of the tree with my still camera. What we wanted to do was turn this black ocean of wild cattle to the camera and film them in a head-on rush. Our professional hunter, Barry assured us that buffalo never charge en masse, only the solitary bulls are dangerous. With this reassurance, we waited next to the dead tree. It was more like a thick bush, barely enough to support a body or two in a pinch. Jack and I measured our distance from this escape route. I calculated I could reach it and climb it in three seconds flat.

Three four-wheel drives circled the herd and started to push them in our direction. The first visual effect was a rolling cloud of white dust. Silent and menacing but as it got closer, the sound effects were added. Heavy black hoofs reverberated the ground like the aftershocks of an earthquake. Sunlight ricocheted off the polished horns of the vanguard. Then the herd hit the grassy soil of the savannah. Like a discarded mantle, the dust remained behind and the individual animals came into sharp focus. Ten meters before our position, the herd opened up like the sea at Moses' command, flowing around us like a thundering flood. On my left Jack was ecstatic. "Fantastic. Unbelievable," he kept repeating as his machine recorded the primordial sight. The bulk of the herd passed, but a group of about fifteen animals was still approaching. Jack stopped filming, but my Nikon was still glued to my eye, snapping stills.

On the right flank, an old cow ran, blowing dust. Through the lens, I could see her eye turning until the brown iris almost disappeared, replaced with a hot white orb. She noticed me and wanted me bad. I dropped my camera but knew my life was finished. No panic yet, just the knowledge of finality. I felt like there was no chance of turning and stepping up the puny sapling. The well-calculated three seconds I did not have. She'll get me before I can turn. The big head is angled to strike, and when she gets to me . . . but she did not. To smash me, she would have had to change course from running straight to curving right, but her speed was too much. If she attempted to turn, she was likely to fall. She ran by five feet from me, hitting me with a flying piece of hard dirt. Somehow, hay-eaters menaced me more than carnivores.

From location, we returned to base camp and Margo and Heather. We tell our stories at the blazing fireplace at the lodge. She sits next to me, shaking her hair, tinted red from the flames. Later, she comes to my room, but once again I am told this is an exception to finish a pleasant evening. "I'll never be your girlfriend." Happy with the present, I assure her that it would be far from me to seek a serious or long-term relationship. Carpe diem: enjoy the day and the body you are with. On this light note, she returns to her room at dawn, leaving a scent of sandalwood and a few golden hairs on my pillow, but, of course, my heart is untouched.

In the next episode, Lolita, my leopard, had an important role, stealing sheep, attacking a herdsman, and falling into a pit trap. The herder is me in black and white face stripes and an afro fright wig. Jack renamed me Queequeg, the Maori spearman from *Moby Dick*. When I saw the slide he took, I had to agree. The attack starts from a yellow-barked fever tree: Lolita leaps to the scrap of meat hidden in my hand. Her impact knocks me down, and she stays with me for fifteen seconds mouthing the hidden bait. Cut and repeat as usual. Let's give enough footage to the editor.

Lolita attacks

Leopard attack

As a sheep thief, she got carried away; the scene was too realistic. She flattened herself outside the thorn fence, hiding behind a tuft of grass, taking short, fast steps interspersed with frozen minutes of waiting. The final rush took us all by surprise. A flash of yellow, and she had a ewe by the throat. The thick wool is good protection, but I must hurry before she does cut through it to the flesh. I approach her with the calling spoon full of meat to make a trade, but no dice. Eyes tightly shut, she hangs on to the catatonic sheep. I put the leash around her neck and pry her jaws loose. The lucky lamb jumps up and runs back to her flock.

To finish the episode trapping the "spotted killer," our staff dug an eight by four by eight-foot pit, covered with branches, leaves, and grass just like a real poacher would do. Normally, an assistant trainer releases and I call, but Lolita is an elderly leopard, and I do not trust her with anyone. I smear some ground meat on the start point and run to point B, at the opposing edge of the pit. She comes to my call, hits the treacherous surface, falls in for a fraction of a second, and pops out like a champagne cork. "We have to repeat it. It was too short," complains Jack. I have serious doubts about take two after she was tricked, but my policy is never say no to a director, so we try again. She came faster and ran across the pit on a branch no wider than my wrist. The agility of a leopard is next to miraculous.

In the next segment, Lolita had to be in the same shot with an African boy about eight years old. Somehow, the movies insist on mixing children and big cats, a dangerous combination. Lolita was to lie in wait on the thick branch of a fever tree while the herd-boy walks by. For safety I put a two-millimeter cable around her neck and held on to the end of it. Thank God. She picked her moment and sprang in the boy's direction, but the cable stopped her and cut a deep groove in the tree bark from the force and speed of her leap.

By the end of April, the drought had ended and nature recovered with amazing swiftness. The lifeless brown grass and trees turned vivid green practically overnight. The rain brought on the spectacle of termites. Swarming by the millions, the insects leave the dark interior of their castles, providing a feast for a multitude of birds and beasts. The elegant fish eagles looked ridiculous hunting for insects. Hopping on yellow feet, they looked like a midget on a bicycle.

Susan Dey, of the *Partridge Family* TV show, came out as the guest star of the next episode. She played an aviatrix who crashes in the hostile desert of Northern Kenya. A spitting cobra nearly blinds her. Cape hunting dogs close in on her; "Lassie," beg your pardon, "Elsa" comes to her rescue. What an original plot.

We borrowed a pack of six hunting dogs from the Nairobi Game Park. The scene was filmed in an enclosure so that we would not lose any of these "painted wolves." The line producer, Paul Radin, showed up to witness our efforts. Wisely, he stayed on the safer side of the fence. My first lioness, Arusha, walks around nonchalantly, unaware of the dogs separated from her by a wooden door. Jack had enough footage of Elsa meandering and yells, "Turn them loose." The pack leaves their den, sniffing the air. Then, like struck by a bolt of lightning, the leader, an old bitch, stiffens and gives a warning whoop to her subordinates. With excited chitter, they start milling about, picking up the scent of the lioness. Coming over the granite boulder, they make visual contact and flow down the slope. Like pestering flies, they surround the peaceful big cat. She looks back over her shoulder and keeps on walking.

The dogs start yelping and snapping, giving courage to each other. It is like a medieval tapestry coming to life or the Roman Colosseum. The producer is watching from the safe side of the wire. He is completely involved, with the perspiration from his forehead dripping on to his horn-rimmed glasses. Like Indians attacking a wagon train, the dogs run circles around the lioness. Tails erect, some even stand on hind legs, tightening the circle. Arusha is not amused at this brazen behavior. She rushes at the dog closest to her with a full throttled roar. For a few seconds, she silences her tormentors. She wants to be alone.

Like street thugs mobbing a solitary pedestrian, the "painted wolves" regroup and catch up with her. She whirls and scatters them in six different directions, but the matriarch rallies her pack. The circle reforms, and the bravest hooligan grabs the tufted tail of the lioness. A fatal mistake. Arusha's response is the instinctive spark of a million years of evolution. Her body bends in a tawny arc. Forearm, with razor sharp claws extended, connects with the dog and yanks it to her roaring mouth. The movement is so fast and coordinated it seems like the dog voluntarily jumped between the open jaws. Like a giant nutcracker, he crunches the vertebrae. Fred and I jump in at the same second, but human speed is too slow for nature's killing machine. Arusha releases the twitching body, and the dogs retreat with their tails at half-mast.

The scene played with too much cinema verite. The producer pries his fingers from the wire fence, and, with sagging shoulders, returns to his air-conditioned car. I do not envy his task. He has to explain to the director of the Nairobi Game Park the missing dog. The rest of the episode we film at Lake Rudolph. Our caravan takes off at the crack of dawn. At the town of Nakuru, we leave civilization behind. Miss Dey is riding with me. We discuss politics, African natives, and over-population and politely disagree on everything but the classical tapes playing on the car stereo.

Our camp manager, Barry, left two days ahead of us. Tents welcomed us when, at midnight, we finally arrive at our destination at Loyongolani. My tent is just steps away from the lapping waves of the lake discovered by my countryman, Samuel Teleki, in 1888. Like most early explorers, Uncle Samuel wasn't stingy with the gunpowder and shot his share of game and recalcitrant natives. After independence, Lake Rudolf was renamed Lake Turkana after the predominant tribe of the area. The tribe living on the shore is the El Molo, one of the smallest tribes in Africa, numbering only a few hundred and existing on fish and crocodile meat. If I were an El Molo, I'd move to another region of this vast continent, I mused as I listened to the incessant rustling of the palm leaves in the strong wind that blew all night. Finally, exhaustion takes over, and I submerge in a sweaty sleep.

Jack likes to start early, but in this climate early is a relative concept. At 8 a.m., the temperature reached 109 degrees Fahrenheit and my usually reliable lioness, Arusha, is dazed in the merciless heat. At 10:30, we have to stop filming. Instead of coming to my car, she turns and walks the other direction. Her expression is totally vacant. She is not defying me; she is just numb from the infernal heat. When I catch up to her, she refuses to be offered water. The only thing to do is stop filming for the day. We while away the time at the hot spring, Loyongolani.

Even this harsh climate has attraction for some people. At the bar, we meet Rodney Elliott, one of the legendary game wardens of the good old days. Rodney told us a couple of amazing crocodile stories. The lake has a large population of these leftover dinosaurs. Rodney was building a jetty reaching a hundred feet into the frothy waves. The work went on smoothly for days, and the crew was getting careless when a giant reptile grabbed one of the workers, a six-foot-two turkana. One second he was nailing planks to the pilings, and the next second he disappeared in a swirl of water. A minute later, the attacker surfaced from deep in the lake with his victim's legs between his jaws. He swallowed the native in one piece. The next week, Rodney was approaching the ill-fated jetty by boat when a medium-sized croc about three meters long slid off the sand bar and swam toward them with murder in his beady, black eyes. He was gaining against the puffing motor, and when he snapped at the side of the boat, Rodney had enough and shot him. When examined on the bank, they found a rusted El Molo harpoon in his groin. No wonder the poor reptile was anti-social.

In the evening, around sunset, we were enjoying a gin and tonic at the bar when a light plane buzzed us. The pilot dips the left wing, and someone with blonde hair is waving at me. I'd recognize that mane anywhere. Heather, my lioness, is flying up there. The plane makes one more circle and drops a note.

"Spent the weekend in Marsabit. Miss you. Kwa-heri. H." I slept with the note. It kept me smiling during the noisy whisper of the palm trees.

In the next two days, we managed to get enough footage, despite the brutal heat, and returned to base camp in Naivasha. The first person to greet our dusty caravan was Heather, all smiles and radiance. She told me she was bored to distraction being the secretary of a mumbling producer whose main occupation was solving crossword puzzles. "Could you arrange for me to switch over to the lion department as a keeper? I'd be very grateful." She punctuated this sentence by drawing her tongue over her lower lip. There is no fool like an old fool trying to please a young maid.

The first answer to my inquiry with the management was, "Are you out of your mind? She has never handled a dog before, never mind a lion, and besides, she is needed in the office."

"To help with the crossword puzzles," was my reply. "I have been watching her, and she definitely has animal sense. That is the most important aspect of any training. Besides, I am good enough to make a lion tamer out of practically anybody."

"Especially if she is your girlfriend," remarked Jack with a large dose of sarcasm.

"My girlfriend she is not, unfortunately," I said firmly. The end result: Heather started as a keeper the next morning. I put her in charge of two cubs, Sparky and Sunshine, whose personalities matched hers and Margo's. For me, the happiest part of the year commenced. While her attitude of "I'm not your girlfriend" did not change, we spent a lot of time together officially and privately. She moved into the lion camp, and most nights I ended up in her tent, with its tasteful femininity and minus the photo of the Italian. That picture was never seen again.

On the weekends, the four of us took mini safaris. As an additional advantage, I was driving an action vehicle for the show that bore the logo "Kenya Game Department." The guards at the gate of the Nairobi game Park looked at us suspiciously—like "what are this paleface and the blonde doing in an official vehicle?"—but when both of us started to speak Swahili, the gates were opened followed by a snappy salute. On one occasion, a smart aleck remarked, "There are no more muzungus, white men, in the Kenya Game Department." He was overruled by his sergeant, "Lakini pesa yangu atakuja, Uleya." Your money is still coming from Europe, "Kumbafu," idiot.

The phony film logo also saved me from a stiff fine. No one is supposed to get out of a vehicle in a game park for safety reasons. But the best animal photos are taken from the animal's eye level. I was on my stomach, snapping away at the wildebeest reflected in the setting sun, when the game warden flies over us, but when he saw the logo, he dipped his wing and flew by.

Heather was becoming more familiar with the lions. On a slow morning, we were getting ready for a practice session, chatting before the gate. Something made me look back over my shoulder, and there she was, leading Asali, my prize lioness, all by herself. I didn't know whether to praise her or to chew her out for taking unnecessary risks. I ended up praising her. My pupil. Being a lion tamer is more exciting than being a secretary.

On occasion the work gets a bit too exciting. The script called for a pair of lions stalking game. The ever-useful Crescent Island provided the backdrop. During my filming in Africa, I worked with nine males and fifteen lionesses. The lionesses were always ready to hunt, given a chance, but on this occasion nobody wanted to chase the game. Asali came into heat. She can do this at the drop of a hat, and she suddenly decided to get amorous after I let her out of the Land Rover. She flopped down in front of Hatari like a Hollywood starlet wanting a part. Lions are very serious, sometimes deadly serious, when it comes to love. The best-natured lion can become a raging monster if he feels someone is trying to keep him from the object of his desire. This was also true of Hatari, who had a dark side to him to begin with.

The scene was set up inside an electric fence, but only the camera crew was on the outside. The trainers' work was inside. As soon as I approached Asali, Hatari came for me in short, stiff-shouldered bursts. My local helper, Alex, found this too much and, like a big grasshopper, jumped over the wire to safety. My true backup, Fred, was at my side in a flash and shot a cold white cloud of CO_2 at the charging lion. He retreated and crouched behind a log, fixing us with yellow eyes burning with jealousy. There was only one choice, to collect Asali. She played coy with us for a while, rolling and making sexy groans, but then suddenly she leapt up and came to me. I gave Hatari ten minutes to cool off, then collected him as well.

Heather went to the coast with her family. On Monday she was looking at me with an expression I couldn't quite read. Little by little, reality came to the surface. Over the weekend she met another Italian, a rocket scientist no less. Even for a person with a lot of self-control, jealousy is probably the hardest emotion to control, and the green-eyed monster was surely blinking under my calm surface. For two weeks our relationship was hobbling along, then it improved. No explanation, but I suspected the rocket launcher got out of the picture.

With time, the scripts got worse, not that they were really good to begin with, but we still got visiting VIPs from NBC and Columbia Studios. The president of NBC graced our compound with his presence. Heather was leading the delegation from one lion to the next. She was telling them about Blake, the wrestling lion, and how cold and indifferent he was. Blake might not have liked what he heard. In his underhanded fashion, he got up like he was bored with the world, and especially with studio executives, and sprayed the big man from head to foot with his caustic yellow urine. The president laughed, at least on the outside. A week later, a telegram came from the same executive, "While the ratings were okay, they were not high enough for the most expensive show on the air. At the end of episode twelve, the show is cancelled. You all did an exceptionally fine job. See you on our next project." Well, maybe he did get mad at Blake pissing on him.

There is a strange mood at the end of a film, but this time it hit some of us harder than others. The leading man, Garry Collins, and I took it the worst. A run of three or four years would have been just fine with us. Heather was of the same opinion. Now that the end of filming was approaching, our relationship took a new turn for the better. The rocket launcher disappeared, and we spent more time together. The result was that I truly and deeply fell for her. Something I denied but she predicted long ago. She even called me her boyfriend to an acquaintance. It made my heart sing.

Once a production is doomed, the nickel counters step in with ruthless efficiency. Now every penny is of importance. The lions have to be returned to California with the greatest of speed. Fred traveled with live cargo while I decided to stay three weeks longer and go on a final safari with my blonde lioness. She called it, with Kenyan humor, a "perversion excursion." On a gorgeous tropical eve, I took a picture of her and Asali. It was the best shot of my life. The magical light of the African sun painted the golden-haired girl and the tawny lioness with a diffused halo of red, yellow, and sentimentality. I had two copies made, but she lost the negative.

Our safari started in Nairobi at the New Stanley Hotel. The phone rang at the ungodly hour of 7 a.m. It was her mother asking for her daughter, who was waking up next to me like a sleepy kitten. The venom oozing out of her voice should have warned me, but like a fool I said, "Yes, she is here," and handed her the receiver. Mommy dearest wanted to discontinue our safari before it started, but her daughter firmly refused. She wasn't overly fond of her mother. "Father should have been more careful before picking you," she hissed before slamming down the phone.

While the incident was unpleasant, it was also encouraging: Heather stood up for me and our final safari. By now, I knew and admitted that the lightning bolt had struck me. I was agonizingly in love. This was no surprise to her; she had warned me long ago. For the final leg of our safari, we went across the border to Arusha, in Tanzania. Here, at the foot of Mt. Meru, stood a lodge as beautiful as an old-fashioned movie set, and here she met a young, professional hunter named Andy.

In the evening, around the crackling fireplace, an international crowd gathered: hunters, botanists, naturalists, and just plain tourists. A card game started, and I found myself with four others in this seldom-pursued pastime. And, to my surprise, I was constantly and almost embarrassingly winning. The pile of matchsticks, our currency, was getting higher and wider. Lucky in gambling, unlucky in love goes the saying. At the next table, Heather and Andy were playing an ancient African game called Bao. The base of this very complicated game is a hardwood board with parallel indentations, about twenty-four. The players move shiny pebbles from hollow to hollow. My eye wandered from the card game to Heather and Andy as they played the ancient game while an even older game was developing. His hand touched hers, and I saw my doom in this slight movement.

That night, her affection evaporated, and she actually said the ominous four words: "We have to talk."

"I know. I have seen it. You are in love with Andy."

She just nodded, confusion showing in her shiny eyes. What can a man say in a situation like this? We agreed to continue our safari, only four days left, and then she would return to Arusha to be near her devastating new love, the young hunter. The next night we spent in a small cabin on Mt. Meru. The setting was ideal. Giant moss-covered trees, brooks leaping from stone to stone. At night, our mood turned malleable. I knew that this was one of the last nights I'd spend with the woman who finally made me understand what falling in love means.

My mood took swings like the pendulum of doom, chiming occasional unreasonable hope dashed by bitter jealousy. The logs crackling in the fireplace reflected visions of souls burning in the torment of rejected emotions, and out in the primordial jungle a green-eyed demon rode on a rogue elephant, trampling over beautiful memories of the past. In a bizarre move, I hid her lingerie under the mattress, hoping that when she spent a night in this enchanted cabin, perhaps her lover would find the pink garment and the memory that I was there would come back to haunt them, at least temporarily.

We left for Nairobi. Two days until my departure to Europe. She consented to spend the last night with me at the hotel. This time Mommy dearest did not discover our cooled off love nest. She enjoyed the night, but in the morning felt guilty. The big brown eyes of Andy hunted her. As my last loss of the day, she misplaced the negative of her and the lioness in the golden light on the lakeshore. Even the most perfect picture I took expired. She signed my only copy "Kwa-heri"—"until I see you" in Swahili. I hoped she'd hang around until boarding time, but I did not get that favor. She told me about a dream she had about flying to Arusha. The plane got into a storm and crashed. "I am afraid I will die in a crash and never see him." Shortly after finishing this dramatic story, I received a hurried kiss. She jumped into her VW bug and left forever out of my life. I thought. Her scent, Miss Dior, lingered on my lips until, like a zombie, I boarded the plane. In Vienna, my former classmate, Imre, picked me up. His first remark: "You look like a ghost."

"No, this is worse. Ghosts have no heart, feel no pain."

"Well, tell me about it."

I spent December in Europe. My first Christmas with the family since 1955. My mood matched the gloomy climate, but deep down still a flicker of hope slumbered. And then the letter with the colorful foreign stamps arrived. "I am so happy you introduced me to Andy. He is everything I ever dreamed about. Gentle, considerate, and a good lover." Of all things, this thorn stuck the deepest, past the heart.

In January I returned to California to my newly built home, up until now seen only in Polaroid shots. The letters kept coming from Africa. Things were still ideal in paradise. "He is incredibly brave. He was attacked by a Cape buffalo, and his gun-bearer saved him." Et cetera. It still hurt, but the wound was not bleeding anymore. The experience gave me the idea for my first script. And then the phone rang. An Italian company wanted a chimp for a jungle adventure starring Juliano Gemma. Juliano who? Well, he is famous in Italy. The Italian Rock Hudson, except he likes women. The leading lady was the original Bond girl, Ursula Andress.

Ricky and Ursula Andress

And they would film in Africa. My heart started beating faster, but the location wasn't Kenya, but in war-torn Rhodesia. Yes, I am politically correct. Zimbabwe in 1975 was still Rhodesia. I bought a six-year-old chimp named Ricky. He knew very little and wasn't a simian Einstein, and I had no trouble taking him over. Ricky and I took British Airways to Jo'burg to Bulawayo to Victoria Falls.

My chimp was housed at the back of the old Victoria Falls Hotel in a laundry room. My quarters looked at the falls: "Moshi o Tunia"—the smoke that thunders, as the Africans call it. In the script, Ricky was the pet of Senor Gemma, the Latin Rock Hudson without the taste for young boys but also without Mr. Hudson's acting ability. It was never clear to me what role Miss Andress played. At times she appeared on the set as a sexy nun, at times as a sexy prostitute, but in all roles she was Juliano's sidekick and love interest.

Rhodesia in 1975 was in the middle of the war of independence. Understandably, the Africans wanted to take over the reins of their own destiny, and the Rhodesians of European lineage tried to hold onto the reins of power. The result: shooting at each other. Having survived a war and a revolution, the fighting did not worry me unduly, until a few grenades landed on the lawn of the elegant old Victoria Falls Hotel.

One humorous episode was due to the Italian lack of organization. The day's filming involved some shooting. Blanks, of course. As soon as the actors fired some rounds, it seemed that within seconds we were surrounded by the entire Rhodesian Army, but their weapons had live ammunition. "Hands up! Freeze! Don't move!" flew the commands at the pale crew, whose management forgot to notify the authorities about the make-believe shooting. With the help of our interpreter, the situation was explained and the army melted back into the bush, shaking their heads and muttering that the Latins might be good lovers but are certainly lousy organizers. The next day, they forgot to inform the caterer about our distant location. Lunch did not arrive. This time everybody was hopping mad. "No pasta; we are starving to death."

Ricky was not only not too brainy, but he also liked to run. If he thought he was out of my physical reach, he'd take to the trees and do gymnastics for hours. I prevented him from this annoying habit by attaching a short piece of cable to his ankle. This way he felt bound to me even when the distance made me helpless. It also proved that I am smarter than a six-year-old chimp.

Filming came to an end. I was booked Bulawayo-Jo'burg – L.A., only the ticket in my hand terminated in Jo'burg. The producer, Salvatore, assured me that all was under control. "Miss Graciella will be waiting for you with the rest of the ticket." "Tutti Italiani Ladroni"—all Italians are liars, said Napoleon. Tutti no, but this producer was a big liar. In Jo'burg, I found no trace of Miss Graciella or my ticket, but I knew the crew and the producer would follow on the next flight. I ambushed him as he exited his plane and squeezed the rest of Ricky's and my fare out of him.

CHAPTER 14

HAWMPS OR RIDE THEM CAMELS, COWBOYS

Before the civil war, during the presidency of Millard Fillmore, the army tried an unusual experiment. Replace horses with ships of the desert, camels. The director of the hit doggie epic *Benji* based his script on this historical fact. The animal coordinator was the trainer of Benji, the 350-pound Frank Inn. He also played the role of the cook. The large training barn of Jungleland was still standing, and that is where we housed and worked the 16 dromedaries (one hump) and one bactrian (two humps).

Camels are strange animals. Smarter, stronger, and more challenging to ride than horses. Frank picked wranglers with lots of horse experience. I was the only one whose total time in the saddle was less than five hours and most of it on a giraffe. Never mind. I bought chaps and pointed cowboy boots and climbed up

161

on the tall animals. The rest of the trainers were practically born in the saddle. Paul, Fess, and Billy even tried rodeo.

Camels in the US Calvary

My steed, Karthoum, was coming along fine. I out rode a half dozen bucking fits, and my confidence was soaring. A mistake with camels. From a quiet walk, without warning, my mount jumped sky high, and I landed on concrete, my left hand folded under me. Crunch! The x-ray showed two clean breaks, but I continued riding with a cast.

After breaking the camels as individuals, we hooked six and six together for the camel train scene. Cowboy Paul was leading train A, and I was riding the last animal on train B. Suddenly, a camel from Paul's line broke his lead rope and, head outstretched, aimed for me. Grabbing the pommel with my good hand, I prepared to die. The collision and the collapse of the seven animals will surely kill me. Well, it wasn't my time to check out. At the last second, the loose camel stuck his neck out and went under the rope holding my mount to the one in front of me. Phew!

After this incident, Valentine, a six-month-old baby camel, became my main responsibility. She had an important part in the film. Her top trick was to pick up a sasparilla bottle from the table, raise, and empty it. In the bar fight, she'd smash it on the head of a rowdy cowpoke. I was pleasantly surprised at how fast she learned.

For location, we moved to a place called Old Tucson in Arizona. It had a dusty main street, a sheriff's office, and a dance hall for the unavoidable bar fight. We, the trainers, became extras, pardon me, "background artists" to be politically correct, and my cowboy friend taught me an important lesson. Some people, the yellow bellies, run out of the bar at the first throw of a haymaker. Your wages are the same so why stay in the dusty, sweaty room? Sure enough, after the first thirty frames of film, Paul and I hit the batwing doors.

Old Tucson had a gift shop, and one of the tourists helped himself to some knickknacks. The senior owner ran after him, shaking his fist, without a hope of catching him, but the thief was still out of luck. Cowboy Paul happened to ride by and chased the culprit through the chollya cactus infested terrain. The thief was fast but no match for the humpbacked charger. As a final insult, the camel spit his green bile in his face. The villain of the story was played by Jack Elam, a cross-eyed, lanky character actor known for his roles as a baddie. Mr. Elam's stunt double broke most of his ribs in a fall from his camel. The director's finger pointed at me being the same height as the important actor. Survive this I must. It wasn't a very elegant ride, but, after all, I was doubling for the villain. The camel's peculiar shuffle, right front and right hind leg moving in tandem, becomes more difficult with speed, so shame be damned, I grabbed the pommel with white knuckles. "You are very good at pulling wool," said my cowboy buddies, but I stayed in the saddle.

Unlike *Benji*, *Hawmps* was not a box office bonanza. Some animals, like cute dogs, lions, and dolphins, can carry a film, but the smelly, curmudgeonly camel is not one of them. As a historical footnote, the army's experiment with camels was also a failure. Some were turned loose in the southwestern desert and hunted to death in a few years. The Arabian riding instructor Hadji Ali, or as the cowboys called him, Hi Jolly, is resting in Quartzsite, Arizona.

CHAPTER 15

M'ZEE SIMBA, THE OLD LION

A frica is in my blood, and fate has granted me twenty-seven journeys to the cradle of mankind. In 1979, my friend, the director, Jack, got a script by Marshal Thompson, who played Daktari on TV. It was about an old lion on his last leg, too slow to catch game, but he teams up with a greyhound. How did the greyhound end up on the savannah? Well, riding with his master on a light plane, which crashes. Master stays injured in the ruins, but hound goes for help. "Lassie, go get the paramedics." During his quest, he meets M'zee Simba, the old lion.

A colleague of mine, Monty, a fine trainer of cats, had the perfect lion by the name of Zamba. He inherited his animal from the ruins of Ivan Tors' enterprises. I was impressed by how Monty worked him at liberty, and when introduced to the hound, there were no sparks flying. For one episode, we moved to the Maasai Mara National Park, famous for its majestic, black-maned lions.

After a successful day of shooting, we were sitting around the campfire. Flaming branches of acacia wood painted a wide circle of light in the black night. Monty had Zamba staked out to a stump with an eight-foot chain. The fire and gin and tonics did their soporific effect. We all but dozed off in our comfortable canvas chairs when Monty's assistant, Susie, interrupted our peaceful meditation. "Where is Zamba?" Where a few seconds ago he rested on his chin, there was only flattened grass and slack chain. Monty, fine trainer though he was, at times was a bit cavalier with safety and put the chain on too loose. We jumped into three different Land Rovers and took off looking for the missing cat.

The situation was extremely serious. Around us, the wild lions started their evening concert, and if our California lion met one of those battle-scarred warriors, the outcome would be Simba one, Zamba zero. Driving in slow gear, my headlights cut a tunnel through the dark wilderness. About a mile from camp, my lights picked up the shape of a large lion. Positive identification was not possible, but it did not move or run away. About fifty yards away, I got out and addressed the resting cat. "Zamba, on your feet!" He stood up. "Zamba, come here." He slowly moved in my direction. At this moment, doubt raised its ugly head. What if it is not Zamba? What if? I got back into the car, flashed my lights, and shouted louder than the roaring lions. "Monty, come here!" He did, and Zamba obediently jumped into the back of his Land Rover.

According to script, the old lion is bitten by a spitting cobra and buried under a flat-topped acacia laden with bell-shaped nests of weaver birds. For the cobra bite, we used a rubber snake, and, at Monty's command, "Zamba, lie down on your side!" Zamba died convincingly. No one can see into the future. This fine lion's end was even more tragic.

A family came to visit the ranch where he was kept, and a young boy was flying his model airplane without parental supervision. A sudden gust of wind swept the glider into the compound. The child, eager to reclaim his prized toy, lifted the wire far enough to crawl into danger. This was temptation no big cat could resist. Zamba pounced and killed him. When the police arrived, he was still guarding the cold body, and the officers shot him, not having much choice in the matter. Yes, tragedies do happen in our vocation. On average, a human is killed or seriously injured by a lion, tiger, bear, or elephant about every five years. The reason, quite often, as in a plane crash, is human error, but sometimes it happens because a lion is a lion and a tiger is a tiger, ruled by eons of reflexes lurking under the surface.

One of the better known accidents was Roy Horn of the Siegfried & Roy magician duo. I had not seen it happen, but I heard that Roy slipped, and that was enough for Montecore, his tiger, to drag him backstage where the safety crew freed him. Roy was a very good animal man. The only thing I would have done different is to have safety equipment on stage. The seconds it took the cat to drag him backstage must have been eternity and made the damage more serious. What I did not agree with, and sounds totally false, is what the publicity man released to the press. "Montecore did not want to hurt Roy. He was trying to save him." Save him from what? No, he tried to kill him, and if given a chance, probably devour him al dente.

Are accidents, as some on the extreme right of the animal protection industry suggest, reason enough to put a group of highly trained and motivated professionals out of business? I think not. We decide to make our living with potential danger, and something drastic can happen every day of our life, yet we take the risk. Some critics say we are not supervised and regulated enough. When I had my motion picture animal farm, I was inspected seven times—as often as a human daycare center where abuse can easily happen to children.

From the federal government to the state government to the local dog catcher, all had a right to show up unannounced, fine me, and, if the complaint was serious enough, revoke my many licenses. Supervision, yes, being hounded to despair, no. There is a tendency in our great country to outlaw accidents. Would it not be a perfect life if we could do that? Unfortunately, this is not a utopia. A state or situation of ideal perfection, unattainable on this planet.

CHAPTER 16

SEA GYPSIES AND *WILDERNESS FAMILY*

The movie *Sea Gypsies* was a wonderful idea written by my tall British friend, Stuart. A bit like *The Swiss Family Robinson*, father, daughter, and young son are shipwrecked on a rocky island off the coast of North America. The menace manifests in the shape of a huge grizzly, trained by the fearless wolverine man, Marinho. The bear, Tag, did his acting inside an electric fence. Two strands of thin wire kept him within the boundaries of the desired scene.

For the chasing the man gag, Marinho filled a washbasin with marshmallows, bread, and fruit, then he would take off as fast as his short legs could transport him. The actor, Bob Logan, ran between Marinho and the bear, from time to time looking back at the advancing carnivore. Tag was gaining on the humans. The wire and safety were within thirty feet. At this point, Marinho threw the basin up in the air. It flew like a mini flying saucer, then, obeying the law of gravity, it

169

landed in the actor's unwilling arms. Bob dropped it like it was radioactive and slid under the fence, joining Marinho.

On this show, my big stunt was being chased by a musk ox. This hairy creature is a survivor of the last ice age. Our Neanderthal ancestors hunted them at their own risk. Like so many of the male herbivores, when raised in captivity the bulls become extremely dangerous. This shaggy beast lived at the Okinagan game farm. The owner took us to his pen, and he nailed me with his beady eyes from the first second. He followed us inside the fence with a deep growl I have not heard from any animal before. It was a steady deep rumble with only one meaning: "I want to kill you. Not just scare you or maim you, but kill you." Well, tomorrow I'll have to be on the other side of the wire. I stay away from sleeping pills on principle, but this evening I took a full Valium. A sleepless night would have been worse.

Morning arrived whether I wanted it or not. The cameras set up on the safe side of the fence, but I had to climb over and face what I get paid for. The bull's attitude was, "Why waste energy if I cannot trample this brazen human who ventured into my territory?" I had to get closer and closer, stomping my foot and throwing ancient insults at him in my native Hungarian. Finally, he judged the distance favorable and took off like hairy lightning. I jumped behind a tree. It was a tall pine, and when he smashed into it, the very top shook like it had Parkinson's disease. I turned and ran for the fence, my oversize rubber boots not helping any, but I made it and dropped to safety on the outside.

"Very good," said the director. "But we need more footage."

Enter the arena I did without voicing the famous gladiator quote: "Morituri te salutant." If your Latin is rusty, it means "Those who are about to die salute you." Two more takes. The bull hits the tree. I run for the fence and climb it. On take four, I got over confident and did not go to the top. A mistake. He raised up on hind legs and hit me in the back of the knee. It wasn't serious, just a short stabbing pain, but I had enough. Luckily, the director had enough footage too. If you rent the *Sea Gypsies*, watch for the hairy beast that nearly put an end to my career.

My next assignment was very similar: *Mountain Family Robinson*. Bachelor father escapes the rat race of the metropolis and searches for peace and solitude in the woods of the West. For a change, he had an eight-year-old son, charming on screen but terror on the set. Even a young actor like Ham, short for Hamilton, figured out that once established, and after a couple of weeks' work in the can, you can throw your weight around.

It was the garden scene. The family busily digging and hoeing to raise fresh vegetables. To make the chores go faster, they sing an inane little ditty. "Put a little seed in the ground . . . etc." Our child participated with a bored mien twice, then just stood resting on his hoe. Director Jack asked him nicely, being a patient man with kids and animals, but Ham wasn't in a giving mood.

"I already sang the stupid thing twice. How many times you want to hear it?"

"But Ham!"

Our pint size thespian turned his back and walked off the set. The six-foot-four director finally lost his patience and grabbed him by the shoulder. The results surprised all of us. Ham turned with the defiance of Humphrey Bogart.

"F-ck you, Jack. Where are you going to get an eight-year-old kid who looks like me?" Touche!

CHAPTER 17

RASING DAISY ROTHSCHILD OR THE LAST GIRAFFE

D id you know that giraffes have seven neck vertebrae like us humans, but this never came up in the movie. Betty Leslie was born in America. She married a British aristocrat, moved to Kenya, acquired a third name—Mellville— and wrote a book about a giraffe subspecies called Rothschild. The reason for naming a long-legged ungulate after a financial genius is unknown. Jock Rutherford was Kenya born, Kenya bred, strong in the arm, and weak in the head. Not reckless but brave to the point of foolishness. Jock's grandmother was one of the few female white hunters, or, to be politically correct, "professional hunters," but she was also white and a crack shot. Jock learned to shoot from Granny.

"Boyo," she would say, "do you see that fence post yonder? Hit it." Jock fired, and dust flew from the assaulted timber.

"Very good, boyo. Now, when you grow up try this." She squinted her blue eyes, took aim, and ping went the barbed wire between two poles.

"In case you think it was an accident, I'll do it again!"

After the war, Jock managed ranches, drank a lot of beer, and in his free time caught giraffes, then he drank some more beer. After independence, the land-hungry population demanded land, and the home of the rare giraffes was cut into subsistence farming plots. This meant the wildlife had to go, either into the pot or relocation.

In the 1970s, there were about one hundred eighty Rothschild's giraffes in Northern Kenya. Giraffes, especially the young ones, do not tolerate tranquilizer well, so they had to be caught the old-fashioned way, with a rope from a moving vehicle or from horseback. The home range of the Rothschild's was not suitable for cars. The waist-high grass was mined by deep burrows dug by ant bears. This curious specialist of nature dines exclusively on termites. With his sickle-like claws, he can dig a man-size hole in minutes, very harmful for axels and horses legs.

Jock Rutherford solved this by depending on his mount's sharp eyes and instincts. Safety helmets were for dandies. His capture equipment was a bamboo pole and a noose at the end, ala John Wayne in *Hatari!* Jock caught Daisy, the heroine of Betty's book in 1976. She sold the film rights to CBS, and the well-known director of nature flicks, my friend Jack Couffer, was picked to helm the project.

The Melvilles' colonial mansion served as the background for some of the action. A mistake as it turned out. Me and my assistant, Gwendolyn, a former student of mine at EATEM (Exotic Animal Training and Management) in Moorpark, California, were given an apartment downstairs. We even had our own household help, a distinguished Kikuyu gentleman. He was so diligent, he locked himself in while he cleaned our rooms. The next morning he did not show up for work. A bit suspicious, Gwendolyn and I checked our cash and valuables. It was all gone, money and even my Acura watch. Without much hope, we called the local constable. He interviewed us, took some notes in his book, and finished with the following, "When you come back to Kenya, bring me a present."

After building stalls for the long-necked actors, Jock Rutherford and his assistant saddled up. In a week we heard the news: "Your first giraffe is ready to be shipped. It is a six-weeks-old girl." Gwendolyn and I drove to the northern town of Eldoret. We named the delicate 450-pound girl Mimosa. Giraffes are one of the few animals with a sweet breath, and when she exhaled it smelled like this exotic yellow flower. She was too young to stand in a crate for the long journey. We marched our baby into the back of the minibus. Two Africans kept her on the back seat while one was holding her head up. Our chauffeur drove as fast as a minibus can go, but we had to stop at the police checkpoints. We had a thick file of permits, but the lawmen was not interested in our captive. "But what about the African population?" they asked.

We made it to giraffe manor. Mimosa took to the bottle, and for a week she seemed to adjust, then her condition started to decline. The local vet had a lot of practice with cows and horses but was only guessing about Mimosa. At the end of the second week, she closed her long fringed eyelashes forever. We all took it hard, especially Gwendolyn, who felt maternal responsibility toward her.

Rutherford made another catch. A male about the same age as Mimosa, but I asked him to deliver the new one to us. Betty named him John Paul after the popular Polish pope. Unfortunately, blessing did not come with the name, and his long-necked holiness died in two weeks. I was shocked, Gwendolyn was heartbroken, and the director worried about the project. The Melvilles hated me.

The show must go on. Rutherford saddled up and soon delivered Rothschild Number Three. The production company flew in a zoo vet from London, one familiar with wild animals. He drastically changed the formula. Giraffe's milk has a much higher fat content than cow's milk. He had us add cream and our new Twiga, Swahili for "giraffe," thrived on it. Betty used to come and visit our new charge just as she did the previous two. She'd sit on top of the corral, let Twiga suck her thumb, and offer carrots from her mouth. I asked her to desist. This animal did not need more human contact, thus more stress than was absolutely necessary. Our relationship got even worse when I asked her not to mother the animal. "Please just stay away."

After the tragic beginning, filming went fairly well, but the story needed some excitement. A lion sequence. My beautiful lioness, Asali, flew across the ocean once more. Her job was to rush into the horsemen about to start the giraffe chase. This was her specialty. Zebras or horses no lion can resist, not even a third-generation California-born lion. She took off like an amber rocket, and by the time the surprised horses could react, she was among them. She picked Jock's mount, leaped, and her front paws hit the saddle. She slid off the target, and the horse took off faster than anything at Ascot. I collected her without any trouble, and for a few days I was treated like a hero. A pleasant change.

A few personal observations about our hosts, the Melvilles. There is no doubt they meant well, but the sad truth is that saving four or five members of an endangered species is less than a drop in the ocean. Does it make you feel better? Of course. As Betty put it, "We stand on moral high ground." Granted. Also, the byproduct of saving wildlife is considerable. New Range Rovers and shiny airplanes all come out of the donations. I owned a fifteen-year-old Land Rover in Africa. It served me well, but I paid for it the old-fashioned way. I earned it.

At the end of filming, the Melvilles told me and Gwendolyn never to set foot on the grounds of giraffe manor, much less enter the colonial brick house, their adobe. I have no desire to do so. I know what is inside. Antique furniture, the smell of old money, and the rare atmosphere of moral high ground would take my breath away.

The critics weren't very kind to our epic. Howard Rosenberg wrote: "The best thing about the *Last Giraffe* is that Marlin Perkins is not in it, lurking somewhere with a lifetime supply of tranquilizer darts ready to immobilize and tag everything that moves. Betty, a photo journalist, had gone to Kenya to do something 'meaningful.' As the giraffe saving heroine, Susan Ansbach, in a Betty Boop voice, cries at the drop of a safari hat while holding forth at her manorial estate in Rodeo Drive-chic outfits, ringing her hands about Daisy. Simon Ward is depressingly amiable as her husband. The pictures are spectacular. The giraffes, loping majestically and Daisy, oh, that face is irresistible."

CHAPTER 18

NEVER CRY "WOLF," BUT BEWARE OF THE DIRECTOR

Farley Mowat's bestseller about a Canadian scientist studying wolves in the arctic was picked up by the Disney Studios. They also picked the latest bright star on cinema's horizon, the director of *The Black Stallion*, Carroll Ballard. I had a meeting with the trainer of the stallion, Corky Randall. He summed up his experiences in one eloquent sentence, "If I never work another day in my life, if my family is at the threshold of starvation, I'd never work with Carroll Ballard again." Corky is as good with horses as a human can get, so I took his words seriously.

That year I had two major motion pictures, *N.C.W.* and a strange road movie, *Honky Tonk Freeway*, directed by John Schlesinger of *Midnight Cowboy* fame. I assigned myself the job of handling a rhino and a waterskiing elephant on *Honky Tonk Freeway*. The stories I write about *N.C.W.* were told to me by my trainers, Cheryl and Richard, the boy from Kenya. Before moving to the wilds of Northern Canada and Alaska, Mr. Ballard had a production meeting, which he opened thus, "I hate horses, I hate wolves, and I hate trainers." Wow! What an excellent way to make friends and influence people!

The human actor was Charles Martin Smith, and I supplied a cast of ten canis lupus, third-generation home-raised arctic whites, blacks, and gray timber wolves. Wolves are highly intelligent, close cousins of the dog, but do not treat them like dogs. Cheryl was in charge of the training. She worked them in a pack and as individuals. Perhaps the biggest obstacle to their education is their built-in wariness of everything new, and in filmmaking every day brings something unexpected.

Three stars of Never Cry Wolf

A magnificent male, Kolchak, became the leader of the pack. I named him after a white Russian general. Unlike circus animals performing in an arena, four-legged actors have to be turned loose on the tundra, return to a call, and get their reward, chicken necks and beef. A certain level of hunger drive is essential to their performance. When the schedule tells you there will be filming on Wednesday and Thursday, you lower the ratio on Tuesday, but to get advance notice from this director was impossible. The trainers took turns to approach him for instructions, and it was Richard's turn to attempt.

Herr Director was enjoying his morning, all organic herbal smoke. He inhaled and said, "You read the book, didn't you?"

"Yes, sir."

"Well then, just be ready for everything in it."

Lucky I wasn't on the job. I probably would have done something physical to Senor Director.

In the twenty-four-hour light of the arctic summer, the trainers worked quite often twenty-four hours nonstop, but after a forty-eight-hour stint, they had enough and went on strike. They joined the Inuit crowd at the Malamute Cafe, drinking Behring bolts, a very potent mix of vodka, rum, and soda. Richard also found unexpected romance in the person of an Eskimo belle. She wasn't built like Nanuk of the north. More like a two-legged fish barrel, and her full moon face was flat like she had been hit in the face with a frying pan. She wanted to take Richard home to her igloo. The polite lad did not say no, just kept buying her shots of Behring bolt until she lost her amorous tendencies.

The trainers' strike ended the next day. The first command from Monsieur Director: "You see that mountain over there?" The mountain was impossible to miss, but it was four miles in the hazy distance. "Never you mind. Here is your walkie talkie, and go." In the high altitude, it took hours to make it to the peak. The radios were silent, so the band of trainers and wolves found a sunny spot under the protection of a rock . . . and fell asleep. Late in the afternoon, still no instructions or even answers to their queries. What can a poor group of abandoned trainers do? They walked back to the truck, but the entire crew had disappeared. The whole climb was just an exercise in directorial revenge for the strike.

For the mob scene of wolves and deer, the production found a huge herd of domestic caribou. Charles Martin Smith was to run with the herd and the predators, naked as a jaybird.

"That is not a very good idea," said Cheryl. "We usually reward the wolves with chicken necks, and we wave it groin high."

The actor wisely said, "I see what you mean. I am going to wear a jockstrap."

The great caribou scene was shot. Hundreds of animals thundered by camera right. A few days later, watching the dailies, the director discovered that all the deer wore a bright red ear tag. Oops! Back to location, but this time film the bloody mob from the right angle. No tags. Near the stampede, a pair of Inuit fishermen were enjoying their whale blubber lunch when they noticed the panicked deer and panting wolves bearing down on them. Into the boat jumps one while his buddy is pushing with all his might. It was a very hard push since the craft was firmly anchored. Besides a whale-size scare, no none was hurt.

Another situation similar to the "You see that mountain over there" happened on the morning of a Nordic whiteout. The swirling mist was so thick it could have substituted for low-calorie sour cream, and Rudolph the red-nosed reindeer would have refused to fly in it. From ten feet, only the black nose of the white wolves was visible.

"I have to have an A to B pass by," growled Comrade Director.

Cheryl and Richard obediently take Kolchak and head for the distant peak. They arrive and patiently wait for the command to "Release the beast," but the radio crackles. "Cut. We got it. Good shot. Come back." The mystery was they never took the wolf off his leash. Carroll Ballard's filmmaking credo was "expose a lot of film, and some of it will be useful."

My friend Jack directed second unit. He was a meticulous planner, practically cutting the material in the camera. When it was time to view the exposed film, Jack's footage was by far superior to what Ballard shot, and he was fuming. Jack was also an associate producer, technically the boss of Comrade Director, yet Ballard had the balls to ask him to cease and desist. The second unit was disbanded.

A key scene in the book and the movie is when the "researcher" and the alpha wolf try to outdo each other by marking their territory with urine. The actor drank gallons of tea, and Cheryl trained Kolchak to lift his leg on command at specific targets. A stunted pine tree, a fallen log, an igloo-shaped boulder. It took fifty-seven takes to satisfy Herr Director's visions.

Finally, after three years and one million feet of film, the same as it took to make *Gone With the Wind*, the material was dropped into the lap of the editor The premiere was in October 1983. In one of the interviews, *Los Angeles Times*,

October 24, Mr. Ballard said, "The wolves used in the movie weren't really trained." Well, Comrade Director, next time you make a movie with untrained wolves, ask the alpha male to lift his leg on command fifty-seven times, and good luck to you.

Richard had the misfortune to work with Commandant Ballard once more. This time in the Namib Desert of South Africa, with cheetahs. This should have been a dream job, but it was not. One morning the tantrums from the leader reached epic proportions. He slammed his safari hat on the sand and jumped up and down on it like an aged Dennis the Menace. To defuse the situation, Richard turned to the assistant director: "For God's sake, somebody rescue that hat. Can't you see he is furious at it?" By the way, this movie turned out so bad it did not even look professional.

While my trainers suffered from frostbite and the unreasonable demands of their Fuhrer, I was getting a deep tan teaching an elephant to water ski. *Honky Tonk Freeway* was a silly road movie with a fine cast, Beau Bridges, Jessica Tandy, Hume Cronyn, Geraldine Page, Teri Garr. All fine actors deserving a better script. The director, also a big name, John Schlesinger. A group of unrelated people, migrating for reasons unknown, to balmy Florida. In the cast were a pair of inept bank robbers, two nuns, a pimp and his bimbo, and a writer with a yarn about a cannibalistic pony.

In Florida, the tiny town of Ticlaw is in danger of losing their tourist dollars. The newly built freeway will bypass their community. The town fathers come up with a solution: we'll blow up the overpass and train an elephant to waterski. What a tourist attraction! Can elephants ski? Wasn't she afraid of water? Some people asked me. Elephants, at certain locations, swim for miles from the mainland of Africa to nearby islands for fun and fresh grazing. My friend, Wally, from Jungleland days put Katy on two giant skis on dry land, running on tracks. All we had to do was just convince her to stay on the contraption, and she skied like a mermaid at Tarpon Springs. Tourist attraction it may have been, but nothing could save this movie. It was a critical and financial sand trap.

Elephant water skis in Honkey Tonk Freeway

CHAPTER 19

SHEENA, QUEEN OF THE JUNGLE, AND FIVE RASPBERRY AWARDS

The sarcastic Raspberries were for worst actress, worst director, score, photography, and worst screenplay. For me and my crew, this yarn about a female Tarzan was sheer fun. The pinnacle of our professional life. The director, John Guillermin, was an ogre to the rest of the crew, but he treated the animal unit with respect and liking.

Kirsty Lindsey in Sheena

From the US we shipped to Kenya an elephant, a rhino, four lions, three leopards, four chimpanzees, three white Arabian horses, and twelve flamingos. Two combination passenger and cargo planes were needed to ferry this menagerie. My rhino, Big H, named in my honor, was a day late. Queen Elizabeth used the same airline, and my rhino was bumped off her flight for safety reasons. The horses were for Sheena to ride after a local artist painted zebra stripes on them. The flamingos were to attack a helicopter. I suggested eagles and hawks as more of a menace, but the scriptwriter knew better, and these fragile, long-necked waders remained the pink Luftwaffe. One more pleasant surprise: on *Sheena* I did not have to fight for every penny. "If you need it, you shall have it" was the surprising answer from the producer, Yoram Ben-Ami.

The compound for the animals was set up in Karen, a suburb of Nairobi, the home of the writer Karen Blixen. John Guillermin, John G. from now on, was an action adventurer or, as some wag remarked, the director of big silly movies like *Blue Max* and *Towering Inferno*. There was something in John G.'s psychological makeup that craved danger and hardship. It cannot be a good product if you did not suffer for it. On location finding, he took over the controls from the bush pilot and did some stomach-churning rollovers. The first assistant director was made of softer material and lost it. "I am a paying passenger. I demand better service." When John G. landed the light craft, the assistant director kept on walking all the way back to London, but this time via British Airways.

John G. disregarded the advice of the local weather experts. The rainy season just before Christmas found us high in the Aberdare mountains, a cloudy, misty place and downright miserable during the rains. The washbasin in front of our tent was frozen solid every night.

The lion and rhino compound was a five-minute drive from my tent. Richard and his African assistant, Boniface, stayed with the animals. The second night, about 2 a.m., I woke to the infernal noise of lions roaring, people shouting, and CO_2 fire extinguishers whooshing. I jump into my Land Rover and stop at the double gate of the compound. It is wired on the inside. I stick my arms through the holes, trying to undo the ties when, to my right, something heavy hits the fence. The chain link bends, and a heavy body crushes through the bush.

Richard comes to the gate, face glowing white in the African night. "Are they gone?" he asks.

"What are they?"

"The wild lions. They have been fighting with your cats for the last hour."

The sun eventually came up, and after several cups of tea in the dining tent, our nerves returned to almost normal.

Tanya Roberts was, and probably still is, a gorgeous woman, but her skills as a thespian leave something to be desired. The day we filmed *Magic Circle* was most remarkable. A Jeep is stuck in the primeval jungle. In it, two helpless city boys, the actors Ted Wass and Donovan Scott. On the hood there are two lionesses, and on the roof, my macho three-year-old lion, Kibor. Sheena swings in on the 4:30 vine, lands on the bonnet, and says in her Bronx accent, "Yo wanna doy?" Translation: "You want to die?" She draws a magic circle in the dust, and that will keep all harm from those within.

Enter my rhino, Big H. A guiding trail is constructed from logs and boulders. For reasons only known to himself, Big H. actually stops at the magic line. My friend, Jack, operating the camera, is beside himself. That is as far as the miracle lasted. Kibor could not resist this monumental wrinkled ass. He leaped off his perch and attached himself to the rhino's posterior. The other lions scatter like sparks from a Christmas sparkler. Big H. nonchalantly kicks Kibor off and heads for the fence made out of sixteen-inch timber. I can judge the strength of an elephant, lion, or even a gorilla, but the brute force of a rhino always surprises me. Big H. broke the logs and trotted out into the jungle.

The chase was on, four vehicles following the fugitive. For our luck, he stayed on the narrow forest paths, perhaps because he was a creature of the open savanna. When my car got too close, he turned and stuck his horn exactly in the middle of the front bumper and lifted the vehicle up three times. As a last resort, we had a veterinarian on the set. He fired his tranquilizer gun with a half load into the gray rump. This gave Cowboy Paul a chance to throw his rope around his neck. The end secured to a bumper, we led him into his shipping crate. His career as a movie actor was finished. A local lad, Roy Carr Hartley, of the well-known game-catching family, drove him to the compound in Nairobi.

Big H. behaved himself on the way down, but when his crate rested on the ground, he broke the first barrier of four-inch steel pipes, shattered the two-inch oak door, and, wearing the frame around his neck, proudly marched into his run. Breaking out of his crate at home gave us no trouble, even a bit of humor, but he flew in the same box from New Jersey to Nairobi, and if he decided to do the same at thirty thousand feet in the air . . . well, that would have been the synopsis for *Airport 1986*.

At the end of the filming, I donated him to the Kenya Game Department. In his reinforced crate, I drove him two hundred miles to the Meru National Park where he joined a small herd of white rhino. Happy end? Yes, for five years, then a group of Somali bandits invaded the park and slaughtered the entire herd for their horns. Rest in peace, Big H., but I don't blame Queen Elizabeth for not sharing the same plane with you.

Sheena's mentor in animal lore was a bona fide princess from Uganda. Princess Elizabeth, if possible, was even less of an actress than Tanya, but she looked regal. The tension between the two "actresses" from silent loathing flamed into verbal fireworks. What made it more interesting, there was a visiting Big Cheese from Columbia Studios, and the sound man recorded it all. The script called for Sheena to touch her stepmother, the shaman, a.k.a. Elizabeth of Toro, but she simply and adamantly refused to be pawed by a commoner.

Tanya cut loose with a string of Bronx curses that made my chimps blush. Elizabeth shut her up with a regal: "You go back to the gutter!"

Tanya walked off the set. "I will not work in the same scene with that bitch."

The work had to be finished. Tall Cheryl was dressed in the princess's leather skirt. Her back to the camera, she still did not look Ugandan. Her hairpiece must have come from the Nairobi 5 &10, it looked so bad. All good things come to an end. The movie premiered in August 1984. John Guillermin looked like a patient in a dentist's office, waiting for a double root canal. The poor man had seen the results in the cutting room. Then came the reviews.

The *Hollywood Reporter*: "Sheena stumbles over dialogue flaws. It is eye popping to see her au naturel, under a water fall, to conduct an extended dialogue with Ted Wass totally in the buff. The result is T&A kiddie pic. Elizabeth of Toro speaks as if she has just stepped out of the Book of Ruth."

The *Los Angeles Times*: "Leave this Sheena to the jungle. It is an idiotic mishmash." The critics were kinder to the animal department.

The same *Los Angeles Times*: "…The animals, however, all of whose training puts almost all of the actors to shame. H.G. Wells has trained them to raze villages, turn over armored tanks and cars, and in the case of the chimps, scamper across the screen with their hands modestly over their private parts. Well, most of the time."

No wonder recognition of my work and a major infusion into my bank account makes me say, "To hell with the critics. Sheena is my favorite movie!"

CHAPTER 20

THE SUNDANCE KID IN AFRICA

All the critics loved Meryl Streep, as they should. She was perfection as Karen Blixen in *Out of Africa*. The role of her lover, Denys Finch Hatton, went to Robert Redford. For me, as a lifelong student of East Africa, this was sacrilege. Denys Finch Hatton was a tall English aristocrat with a bald dome, like the glacier on Mt. Kilimanjaro, while Mr. Redford looked every bit like the Sundance Kid in Kenya. According to office rumor, he received $6 million for eight days of work. Good deal if you can get it.

Somehow, the love story between Karen and her husband, Bror, played better, more true to life. Also true is that Klaus Maria Brandauer acted circles around Redford. Not that he is a bad performer, but Brandauer is simply better. He just did not fit the part, and the part did not fit him. I strayed a long way from my territory, the animal work, but at times I just can't resist the urge to play the insider, the movie expert.

According to Hollywood legend, a relative of Cecil B. DeMille asked him, "How could I be a success in the movie business?"

The great man looked him over and said, "Well, you are not handsome enough to be an actor, not smart enough to direct, but you'll do fine as a producer."

After decades of working with them, I am still not sure what a producer does. Perhaps he talks people out of their money, which is a fine talent indeed, but be that as it may, I had my bitterest moments with these pencil-pushing nickel f-ckers. I described my conflict with the diminutive producer of *Out of Africa* about having sharpshooters on the set. I won. No guns were allowed when the lions worked, and as a parting gesture I picked up the wastepaper basket: "Your work will end up here while mine will shine on the screen as long as there are movies."

I had the best group of trainers to assist me. Cheryl became a trainer at Jungleland, Richard was raised in Kenya, and Doree was one of my students at the Exotic Animal Training program. She spent ten of the best years of my life with me. She was the girl I should have married. She was also a perfect photo double for Meryl Streep. Of the four lion sequences, the first was the most simple. "It is essential that the cat looks straight at Meryl. Can you do that?" asks our director, Sidney Pollack.

Doree Sitterly doubling as Meryl Streep in Out of Africa

I used Asali, my experienced lioness, for the shot. Her mark was a flat stone in the grass. I rehearsed three times, then Asali looked at me with an expression. "I am not an idiot. I know what you want. Let's put film in the camera." For the intense look, I put the tape recorder out of camera range, about the height of Meryl's throat. When the lioness hit her mark, I turned on the recorded roars of a wild pride, and Asali's gaze became questioning and tense.

At the beginning of the hunting sequence, my two male lions, Sudan and Kibor, were feasting on a gnu. Lions, even the ones raised in California, take their dining very seriously. Snapping jaws, claws tearing skin, looked real. For me, the excitement started when the director had enough and yelled cut. I could not let them finish the entire antelope. Satiated, they would sleep for days and to hell with acting. I had to reclaim their prey, but asking Sudan and Kibor to please leave their dinner is not going to work, and force is out of the question. We grab two CO_2 fire extinguishers. On a count of three, we open the foam-belching instrument and rush at the lions. The surprised cats jump up and leave their supper. Richard covers the prey with a plywood. The equilibrium is restored, and we leash up the two performers.

The attack speed required by the director was not easy. The lion's idea of Paradise is to find a zebra within arm's reach, kill it, eat it, and go back to sleep. I needed real motivation to get a convincing charge out of my Hollywood cats. I was lucky. I found Bill Winters, the steeplechase champion of Kenya, and he had the cajones to tease a lion with his horse. I worked out a plan like a chess master before the game of his life. The knight on the board was the brave rider. The queen was Asali in a release cage behind a bush. Bill's horse pranced before her, and on "action," he took off. A second later, I popped Asali's door, and the chase was off . . . or it would have been had I not made a mistake on the side of safety. She bounded out of the box, realized she had no chance to catch the horse, and came back to me.

Sidney Pollack got upset. "What happened? It is costing me $80,000 an hour. I am never going to get this key scene."

"Mr. Pollack," I answered very politely, "I don't care if it is costing you $80,000 a minute. I am working here with the safety and possibly the life of humans as well as animals, and you are going to get your shot."

And so he did. On take three, Asali shifted into high gear and only three feet separated her from Billy's horse, but she lacked that half a second to make the leap. Meryl Streep watched the action from a bullet proof cage. Surprised by the speed, she turned back to the camera and said, "Oh my God!"

In the movie, Redford shoots the charging male lion, and Meryl drops the lioness. I got the effect by practicing the direction of the run for days. Then we dug a fifteen-inch-deep trench across the line of the run and lined the bottom with foam rubber. When the lions running at full speed reached this unexpected barrier, they lost their balance and slid toward the camera, creating the perfect illusion of being shot. The effect was so lifelike that, after the film opened, I got several threatening calls. "I know you killed those lions, and I am going to shoot you!" I still have one of those messages on tape. The lions continued their contented life at my ranch in California.

In the sequence where the lions attack the oxen in the corral, the heroine fights off the intruders with a bullwhip. This was too dangerous for the actors. They were doubled by two trainers: Doree Sitterly for Meryl and Cheryl Harris for the slender Somali lad. After makeup, Doree was such a good photo double that she could be filmed from the front. Meryl showed up two days later for her close-ups, but during the post-production interviews, she described in great detail how she fought off the intruding lions. C'est la vie. Lions in the ox corral was the most exciting part of the movie. Jack ran the camera, and he got every exciting second on film.

The next morning, before Sidney could see the film, the dwarfish producer fired Jack. The script girl, Louise Boyle, handed in malicious reports. Sidney was sorry, but he did not want to counter his production chief. Sidney Pollack was a well-known hypochondriac, and Jack got psychological revenge. He sent Sidney a letter describing in great detail the curse of a Wakamba witch doctor so potent it'll make a voodoo curse look like a blessing by the pope. Sure enough, for the rest of the shoot Mr. Pollack complained about various aches and pains.

Sidney was a very good director, but in Africa he was out of his element. He fell into a mild depression the minute he hit the tarmac at the Nairobi airport. Being a Hollywood liberal, he could not stand the Kenya-born whites, the former colonials. Surprisingly, he thought Africans were shiftless and without humor.

How wrong can you be? No race has a better sense of humor than the Africans, but first you have to get their trust.

The Pollack-Redford team next produced *Havana*. It was so bad Fidel Castro refused to see it. So much for the myth that a big name will produce box office success. All in all, *Out of Africa* was Pollack's best work. Now that he is in the celestial cinema, I hope he gets a front row seat next to Cecil B. DeMille.

CHAPTER 21

OUT OF AFRICA INTO THE FRYING PAN

Project X wanted to draw attention to man's inhumanity to animals. The credits claimed: "Based on a true incident." During the red hot period of the Cold War, the US Air Force used chimpanzees to find out how much radiation a body could take and still drop an atomic bomb on Moscow. The animal work was assigned to a fine trainer, Ron Oxley. In this profession, we are all different, eccentric even, and Ron was no exception. He loved his animals. His lion, Neal, and his bear, Bruno, had free run of his house, and often spent the night with him.

Ron was strong as a mastodon, moody as a witch with PMS, and unfortunately a functioning alcoholic. For *Project X*, he hired three of my trainers, Cheryl, Richard, and Mark. They were prepping at Ron's ranch. He ruled with iron discipline over people working for him. This was in contrast with my work style. My only rule was "I will not work with idiots." The second week into prep, the house was unusually quiet. Richard and Mark did their routine and, at 5 p.m., left for home. After a few miles, Richard said, "I have a weird feeling; let's turn back." They looked in through the living room window. Ron was lying on the floor. The paramedics could not revive him. He had been dead for hours. Since my chimps and trainers were already on the film, Twentieth Century Fox gave me the job of animal coordinator.

African lions were always my favorite, but I had a good relationship with our closest relative, the chimpanzee. The role of Goliath went to my fourteen-year-old Karanja, the veteran of *Sheena* and the Valvoline oil commercial, where for three years he showed the public that changing your oil is so easy even a monkey can do it. The studio also owned two chimps, including Willie, the leading ape, and Harry.

Karanja as a babysitter

Aggression is part of the chimps' social structure and made them a successful branch on the tree of evolution. The recent attacks on humans prove that this cousin of ours can be very dangerous. They fight and bite to climb to the top of the social ladder. At fourteen, Karanja was seven times as powerful as the average human. To out-muscle him would be impossible. My first concern was, like on all my films, the safety of the actors and crew. On *Lance Link, Secret Chimp* I learned an important safety tip from Daryl Keener, the head trainer. The sudden bang of a blank gun is unexpected, respected, and will stop aggression before it gets out of hand. On the days when the large apes performed, I had my .38 loaded with blanks and tucked under my belt, plain for everyone to see. Thank God I never had to use it.

In the most ticklish sequence, Goliath (Karanja) goes ape shit. He had enough of radiation and destroys the office. For good measure, he grabs the cattle prod of an attendant, played ably by trainer-stuntman Fernando Celis, and flings him over a desk. The cattle prod was a harmless prop but later fueled the accusations that we shocked the chimps. It was a remarkable cooperation between human and ape that I could bring Karanja to a fully haired up, swaggering threat behavior without harming Fernando. When the director, Jonathan Kaplan, yelled cut, I told him to sit down and gave him five minutes to cool off. Peace and harmony was restored.

Karanja in Project X

Days later, Willie, the ape owned by the studio, leaped toward Helen Hunt. His trainer grabbed him out of midair and whacked him on the back three times, using about 25 percent of the force his mother would have used in the jungle on a misbehaving youngster. Two weeks later, the same episode was repeated, but now Willie flew at the director's face. Again the trainer stepped in; no damage done to man or beast. At the wrap party, we sliced the cake, drank champagne, and chatted with the two wonderful actors, Matthew Broderick and Helen Hunt. Helen remarked that she was glad Willie did not reach her face. We were all glad.

It was a pleasant party. The relationship between trainers and production was very good, which is not always the case. Jonathan Kaplan is a teddy bear with an occasional snarl. I count him to this day among my few show business friends. I even got along with the two young producers or, as Jonathan called them, "The Boys." We went home with the warm feeling of a job well done. We finished a complicated story with the largest number of big apes without harm to man or ape.

Two weeks later, the fertilizer hit the ventilation system. The two chimps owned by the studio went to a Primarily Primates institute in Texas. I told the studio I could find good homes for them here in California, but the Suits thought it would be good publicity to donate them to a do-gooder organization. As soon as Willie and his companion arrived, the man in charge, Wally Swett, voiced an opinion that these chimps were psychologically abused. The word got back to me, and coming from someone who, to my knowledge, had two years of experience picking up chimp poop, the accusations were infuriating. The same person called and wanted to visit my ranch in California. I politely but firmly said no.

"What are you hiding?" he said in an accusing tone.

"I am hiding nothing. The place is open to any and all inspectors twenty-four hours a day, but if you set foot on my land, I'll pull a citizen's arrest on you." I slammed down the phone.

Mr. Do-Gooder got hold of a well-known talk show host. Let's call him Thomas Torquemada. He had tons of money and influence in local politics. We were not notified but learned from the papers that four of the trainers of *Project X* were facing felony charges. Even the patron saint of all chimps, Jane Goodall, got into the act, but her bad opinion of me did not prevent her from using the adorable portrait of my chimp, Land Rover Smith, on the cover of her brochure. Don't you think, Miss Goodall, it is in poor taste to badmouth someone and later use his pet for your gain?

Land Rover Smith

Torquemada started the steamroller of publicity and the might of the city government against us. We hired lawyers. Mine assured me that if it comes to indictment, he'll accompany me to court and post bail so I will not be paraded handcuffed for the media. Wow! Such legal support really made me feel full of confidence. One of the trainers was recently married. The pressure was so intense that for a while he lost his desire. Luckily, like the entire ordeal, his predicament was temporary.

The tax eaters of the Los Angeles Animal Regulations were mobilized, and we were summoned to Long Beach, facing two interrogators. They behaved so much like the good cop, bad cop from a Hollywood "B" movie that it could have been funny, but it was not. The entire session reminded me of the Spanish Inquisition. Like the victims of it, we were not told who our accusers were or what we were accused of, but the sword of Damocles hanging above our head was very real.

Of course, there were people who defended us, like Helen Hunt and Tippi Hedren. My veterinarian, Dr. Miller, who treated my animals for decades, was my character witness, but most touchingly, was the officer of the Humane Society, the multitalented actor/dancer Gretchen Wyler. In the end, I heard the good news from Gretchen: all the criminal charges were dropped against all the trainers. This was not the very end, but at least the specter of imprisonment passed. The ungodly now tried the easier version of a civil suit. In a short time, this also fizzled. From a distance of twenty-five years, I thought it would be easier to write about this dark period. Easy it was not, but the pain kept flowing the ink of righteous indignation. "The mills of God turn slowly but surely," says an old gypsy saying.

In 2006, the Texas attorney general took control of Primarily Primates after allegations that the place was unfit for animals, and the public donations have been misspent while the animals lived in substandard conditions. A PETA website called Primarily Primates "Hell on Earth for animals." The place was handed over to another institution; the Texas attorney general confirmed that Wally Swett will be permanently barred from the facility as part of the settlement. And Mr. Swett was the man who said that the two chimps of *Project X*, Willie and Harry, were psychologically abused.

Before I finish this chapter, a few words about the Animal Protection Industry, for a lucrative industry it is. On the positive side, we are an animal-loving nation, and there is nothing wrong with that. It is a lot easier to solicit donations with the pitiful face of a stray cat than the photo of a homeless John Doe. As with all charitable organizations, there are some very good ones and some shady ones.

Near Los Angeles, there is a ranch that takes in unwanted pets, domestic and exotic. I heard the following from an employee of this place who quit in disgust. According to him, after one of the seasonal California brush fires, a fawn was delivered to the place. The hot coals of the inferno burned all four hooves of the unfortunate infant to the bone. Help was impossible; the only kind answer was fast and painless euthanasia, but the owner said, "Not so fast. This is Tuesday. By next Friday, I have a fundraiser. She'll be a great motivation for donations." The suffering creature was kept alive for more than a week. If this is not cruelty, I don't know what is. So, dear public, before you send your donations for a swimming pool for orphaned prairie dogs, do like Santa Claus. Make a list and check it twice.

CHAPTER 22

THE CLAN OF SEVEN PRODUCERS AND ONE LONELY CAVE BEAR

Jean M. Auel wrote a wonderful book about the lives of cavemen when the cultures of Neanderthal and Cro-Magnon collided. For someone with imagination, it was like taking a time machine back into the Ice Age about fifteen thousand years ago. The script, also a fine piece of work, was written by John Sayles. The role of Ayla, the willowy long-legged Cro-Magnon, went to Daryl Hannah. James Remar was the leader of the rival, slope-headed Neanderthals. Mr. Remar at first refused to wear the caveman makeup ("My audience deserves to see me as I am"), but one of the seven producers—I don't know if it was Sleepy, Dopey, or Doc—convinced him to turn ugly for art's sake. Fine book, good script, excellent cast. What on earth could go wrong? Well, just about everything.

Michael Chapman, accomplished photographer, took on *Cave Bear* as his directorial debut, and not one, not two, but seven producers held the reins of creativity. Assistant Producer Stan Rogow hired my wolves and my magnificent young lion, Kibor, to be Ice Age animals. I took on the assignment gladly; after all, I took lions and leopards to Africa, and Canada is only next door.

It is not the animals but bureaucracy that poses the first, and usually the biggest, hurdle. Wolves are shot like vermin in Canada, and in Alaska they are hunted from airplanes—just ask Sarah Palin—which I always found very unsporting. They are also on the endangered list. In one state we kill them; in the rest, do not touch them. In short, I needed a federal permit to return them to California. To fly them to Canada, no problem, and all seven producers assured me that, with their connections, the papers would arrive long before my animals finished playing with Ayla. I usually do not believe one producer. Why did I believe seven?

Michael Chapman was looking for locations in lower British Columbia. From the helicopter, he espied a picturesque mountaintop. Canada is full of photogenic mountaintops, but for Chapman this was it. This is where his clan was going to hunt and gather, and no other peak would do. The small disadvantage that this crag could not be climbed by motor car did not bother any of the seven producers; after all, this is not the Pleistocene Epoch. Sikorsky invented the helicopter long ago. "Let there be a cave here on the peak," said the leadership to the construction department, and, duly, a cave appeared made out of fiberglass where only agile marmots lived. Every bit of two-by-four, bucket of paint, turpentine, etc., had to be flown in by whirly bird, and when filming started all humans, wolves, and Andy Gump Porta Potties flew to location every day. Moreover, this mountain was home to some rare alpine moss and lichen. The instruction was, "Do not step on the grass." The actors were the exception. They played their role barefoot, but we who were shod in harder footwear had to walk on prefabricated wooden platforms. A park official watched every move we made.

Key scene. A wolf steals a cave baby. An animated puppet was built at great cost, more than the fee of the live animals and trainers. Cheryl trained Dorka, the large arctic she-wolf, to retrieve. Once she got the idea, she'd pick up your hat, baskets, or the plastic cave child and bring it back to her, but the mechanical infant was a lousy actor. She moved with the jerky gestures of the Frankenstein monster. A blind caveman would have noticed the cheat. "Oh my God! That puppet looks awful," said Chapman. "Bring on another wolf." I thought I did not hear well. The puppet sucks, but it is the wolf's fault?

Kibor the lion played the mystic animal of the tribe. The shaman communicates with him and asks for advice. For this segment, an even more distant ridge was chosen, and I played the shaman. The problem, the large helicopter with the lion crate could not land on this narrow ledge. "Can you take Kibor on leash, sans crate?" This was probably the second bravest or stupidest thing I did since I went back to Hungary for my photos on that Russian-haunted January evening in 1957.

I play a shaman in "Clan of the Cave Bear"

I asked the pilot, "Which one of these wires and pipes is important?" fearing that the lion might panic and claw at the walls.

"I hate to tell you this, but they are all important."

"Okay, Kibor, load up, lie down, and let's go."

We made it. Kibor never moved from his prone position. On the cliff, he came to me. We exchanged Neanderthal wisdom and flew home without an accident. The clan finished acting, the story was in the can, and it was time to go home.

"Producers seven, where are my permits?"

"Ah, the permits. Those permits. Well, we did not get them."

I had my back against the wall of the fiberglass cave. Do I donate my wolves to the local game farm? Do I turn them loose to hunt caribou in British Columbia? Neither solution was acceptable. I had to break the law. Instead of canis lupus, I shipped home five canis domesticus. Five shaggy German shepherds flew to California with the unusual name of Kolchak, Igor, Dorka, Ivan Ruban, and Tovarish. Ivan Ruban was the bully of the pack. At LAX, he jumped at the screen door of his crate and scared the small change out of the cargo handler. "What is the matter with this dog?" Nothing really. He is just mad at some movie folks who lied to him.

The price of the shipping came out of my pocket. The first and only feature on which I lost a considerable amount. The company lost even more. The film was barely watchable. Long-legged Daryl—Ayla—and method-acting James Remar could not save it. My last question: why did we need seven producers? But then, even Snow White needed seven dwarfs to see to her needs.

CHAPTER 23

IVORY COAST, LAND OF BAD JU-JU

The production motto: "Ours is not to reason why, ours is but to do or die." A direct steal from the *Charge of the Light Brigade*. The book was *Sirga the Lioness*, and a French company decided to translate it into moving pictures. In a jungle village, the chief's wife expects twins, but she has only one son, Ule. The jackal, the witchdoctor of the bush, predicts that Owara, the lioness, will have twins, but she has only one daughter. She names her Sirga, after the bright star. Ule and Sirga are born on the same day and become twins in mind and soul. I read the book. Charming story, well written.

The call from the Ivory Coast came at 4 a.m., and two days later I was on a plane to Abidjan. I took a local flight to the town of Man. I met the director, Patrick Grandpierre, and my French colleagues, Guy the snake man, Pierre the falconer, and the big cat man of Europe, Thierry Le Portier. At thirty-nine,

Thierry already had a movie made about his life, and I thought I was doing well when *Life* magazine published photos of my animals.

He was sixteen, attending high school in Marseilles. One day, as he was riding his bicycle, a force grabbed his handle bar, and instead of school he ended up at the zoo. There was a seventy-five-year-old tamer, the French version of Frank Buck, working four lionesses and two leopards. Thierry asked for lessons in lion taming.

"Sure, for $5 a day," said Monsieur Buck.

"Could I be your cage cleaner?"

He cleaned and watched the routine, and, for eating money, he sneaked back at night to the lion house, smuggled two cubs out, and posed them with a pimp and his hoes. At 4 a.m., he took the cubs back to their mother.

The Ivory Coast is not the Africa I grew to love in Kenya and Tanzania. The scenery is more like South America, and the place is ripe with dark magic. The locals were convinced that the crew wanted to sacrifice a girl child to the lions. A colorfully dressed mother showed up with her eight-year-old daughter for a possible part. She walked by the mess tent where the cook was slicing beef for lunch. The mother grabbed her child, and, shrieking, ran down the hill, convinced that her child was the next sacrifice. The assistant director runs after her, and they disappear into the jungle. Two hours later they come back. The mother is holding a strange child from the village as a hostage. Her reasoning: "If you feed my child to the lions, I'll throw this one to them next."

On Monday our driver complained about catching unsavory cooties from the local belles. The staff doctor, whose name was Dr. Fatal, honestly, suggested the use of condoms. On Wednesday he shows up with a pinched face, scratching his crotch. "What is the matter now?"

"This rubber thing hurts like hell. I'd rather have the sickness." He had kept the prophylactic on for two days and nights.

Two blocks from our office lives a Paris-educated lawyer. In the evenings he'd join us at the bar. One evening he showed up with a slight limp. A dog bit him.

"Did you go to the doctor?" Thierry asked him.

"Oh no. I have a friend, a Ju-Ju man extraordinaire. He put some black powder on the wound and bound it with tree bark."

The next day his walk is springy and the bandage is gone.

"That healed fast."

"Yes, and the dog died too, as my friend told me he would."

Today I saw an African youth happily rocking down the main drag, fingers snapping, body swaying to an imaginary tune. His "Walkman" was a piece of wire and two round pieces of wood over his ears. A happy lad he was.

I am very impressed with Thierry's control of his cats. His good reputation is well deserved. Like most trainers in Europe, he uses German commands. They are short and to the point. The African kids picked up his snappy Teutonic words. They chase each other with sticks and holler, "Alle weiter. Du Schwein. On Platz, Ceasar."

On the weekend I talked my friends into visiting a national park. The map showed a large area designated as flora and fauna preserve. We could not find it. There were no signs, no gate, no rangers. The park existed on paper only to squeeze donations out of the gullible public. The next day we met an elderly colonial gentleman at the bar. He was the former manager of the park, but he quit in disgust. The Minister of the Interior uses the park as his own private hunting ground.

I wish I had not gone to the local market. Among the animal products, the saddest was four mummified gorilla hands. The international laws of protection mean little here, but we are very successful in protecting them in Beverly Hills. At least I have not heard of a gorilla being shot on Rodeo Drive.

The Africans renamed Granpier Patrick "Granproblem." He is at the helm, so they blame him for all their misfortunes. Today the entire village was blocking the road to our mountaintop location. They chanted, "No more Mr. Nice Village!" I think. Some had spears, others waved sticks, and the women shook pots and pans at us. The bank did not have enough money to cash the checks they were given for their destroyed coffee bushes and Mango trees.

But the final shady trick pulled by the production company was still to come. The locals built an elaborate set of huts, an entire village, and Granproblem promised they could move in when the filming was finished. There was just one little catch. The last scene is slavers raiding, and they torch the huts. The next day, the whole crew moved to Zimbabwe.

I had some new experiences and am glad I met Thierry, Pierre, and Guy. We trainers should stick together. We drove to Abidjan instead of flying. There was a story floating about Air Ivoire that made driving more acceptable. Up in the air, the captain put his machine on autopilot. He walks into the main cabin and says, "I am captain Gono, and this is my co-pilot . . ." An unexpected lurch slammed the cockpit door shut, and it stuck. Not to worry. One of the seats was loose. The two captains pried it from the floor and busted the door open. Happy ending.

I was hoping to see a gazelle or at least a monkey, but we only saw goats and stray dogs. In Abidjan, I saw the exact replica of the St. Peter's dome built to 9/10 scale. The head of state offered it to the pope, but the Holy Father, after some hesitation, refused it. Why have a replica when you have the original?

CHAPTER 24

THE MAN-EATERS OF
GHOST AND DARKNESS

Vive la Mort, vive la Guerre, vive la Legion Etrangere. The slogan of the French foreign legion, also our motto on the film *The Ghost and the Darkness*. For this project, a truly international cast of lions and trainers was assembled. Thierry Le Portier with Roman and Wotan from France. Mike Hackenburger with Caesar and Bongo from Canada. Brian McMillan with Romeo and Mr. Wells with Sudan from California.

The *Man-Eaters of Tsavo* is the most exciting story of conflict between man and the king of the animals. In 1898, Queen Victoria decided to build a path for the Iron Horse, from the Indian Ocean to Lake Victoria. The adventure of the "Lunatic Railway" has begun. It passed the land of thirst, the Taru desert, and it reached the palm-fringed banks of the Tsavo river. The lions of this region had a bad reputation, and two ugly males, almost bald, started to prey on the imported Indian coolies.

The real man-eaters of Tsavo, in the Field Museum

The man in charge, Colonel Patterson, had his share of trouble with these two connoisseurs of human flesh. Finally, his string of bad luck ran its course and he shot both of them. In 1928, he sold the skins to the Chicago Field Museum, where they still look at the visitors with hungry glass eyes. Patterson's book was the bestseller of his day, and the less changed, the better the script would be, but this did not happen.

The story spent twenty years in incubation, then it was handed over to William Goldman. Goldman is a polished and highly paid screenwriter. He penned *Butch Cassidy and the Sundance Kid* and *All the President's Men*, among many other hits. He reportedly took the job for $600,000 first draft, $400,000 second draft, $1.5 million of the gross, and 5 percent of the profits. For this kind of compensation, he could have written a better script, like the original book. I had a short talk with him on location. He said *The Ghost and the Darkness* idea was given to him by an ancient Maasai on a trip to Kenya. "Bwana, my grandfather, told me about these gigantic lions. One white like the snow on Kilimanjaro, the other dark like midnight in a cave."

The old warrior was lying, of course, hoping for good baksheesh, but Mr. Goldman bought the tall tale, and from the first production meeting on, the Suits tortured us to color our lions. I had some experience on a Japanese film, *The White Lion*. Every morning I sprayed non-toxic streaks and tips on my patient Sudan's mane. We tried the same here. Bongo, the most magnificent, looked like a clown in a fright wig, and Sudan looked like an aging troll. Okay, we'll do it electronically with computers said the wise management. Later, they dropped this idea, and in the film the lions are ordinary, savannah-colored tan.

An East African story should be shot in East Africa, but for financial reasons the studio picked South Africa, which has different vegetation, different soil, but does not have the magical golden light endemic to countries close to the equator. For weeks, semis shipped in the red clay from hundreds of miles and spread it on the ground to imitate the red soil of Tsavo. Our location, the Komati Game Reserve, did not have the required thorn bushes. For weeks, trucks would plant the "impenetrable" thorny barrier of Tsavo. Miles of railroad tracks were laid; the station and the bridge were built to specifications. Movie magic is working. Nineteenth-century railroad cars and a locomotive were also dragged to the set.

The role of Patterson went to Val Kilmer, who took his part seriously. His many pieces of luggage were addressed to "Col. John Patterson," and the same sign marked his parking spot at the dining tent. His living quarters were in the same valley as ours. Green tents on the hillside for the trainers and tents for Mr. Kilmer two hundred yards below us. At the lodge, we had our meals and gin and tonic together. He was interested in Africa, and we had friendly conversations about this fascinating continent. What a nice movie star. Two weeks later, I was summoned to the office. The trainers have to move to town. Mr. Kilmer needs the entire valley.

Val Kilmer in "The Ghost and The Darkness", with Sudan and Myself

"That is very simple," I answered. "Just book the lions and us on the next plane. Two to France, two to Canada, and two to California."

"You don't leave me much wiggle room," said the production manager, and everything remained the same.

At the next gin and tonic session, Val Kilmer apologized for the attempt to evacuate us. "My girlfriend, Cindy Crawford, is coming to visit, and she wants privacy." We promised not to peek, and the friendly atmosphere was restored. I was the only one who did not keep my promise. My tent occupied the highest spot, and a few times I peeked at Cindy dancing around Val's campfire. I was punished for my curiosity with a frightening animal visitation.

I was returning to my tent in pitch dark when I heard the radio knocked off my night stand so violently that the batteries spilled out, rolling on the floor. My weapon, a long flashlight, ready, I jumped in to battle with the intruder. From the dark, a cat-sized hairy monster with eyes big as saucers leaps at me. A bush baby, the screaming ghost of the African night, invaded my canvas home. He bounces on the bed and runs into the bathroom, up on the sink. Toothpaste, brush, and comb fly in every direction. Like a motorcycle artist in the globe of death, he runs on the canvas walls, even on the ceiling, but he cannot find the opening. He knocks the flashlight out of my hand. I find the bottom zipper on the door and open it wide. He finds it and runs out into the night. I take a shower and step out into a soft pile of bush baby shit. I was too tired to shower again. I wiped my feet on a towel and went to sleep.

Thierry's lions look like real man-eaters. Those yellow eyes send only one message: "Come closer, within arm's reach, and you are mine." Bongo and Caesar are useful in the two shots. They are brothers and will not fight. Sudan's role is the all-important physical contact between man and lion. He is our hit cat. Reggie, the lightly built assistant trainer, and myself double in the attack shots. Sudan likes to cream Reggie. On November 2, he did fourteen hits on Reggie and eight on me. Thierry said, "He is working like a machine," which is about as big a

Thierry said he is working like a machine

compliment as I heard from him. I shocked my colleagues when I declared, "There is only one real lion trainer among us, Thierry. The rest of us are clever opportunists."

In a dream sequence, Patterson's wife arrives, and one of the lions kills her. The company found a local stunt girl to double the actress. To gain her confidence, I introduced her to Sudan. "Hand feed him with a piece of meat flat on your palm, like giving a sugar cube to a horse." On the second try, Sudan bit her, so the role of Helena went to Reggie. For eight hours, he wore a frilly nineteenth-century wedding dress. Of course, we teased the daylights out of him, but the $2,000 for the stunt was worth it, he said.

Every member of a film crew is convinced that his job is the most important to success. The makeup artist, the wardrobe person, the prop man, even the animal trainers think that their part is vital. Actually, this is a good trait, which compels everyone to give their best. In *The Ghost and the Darkness*, one gory scene takes place in the hospital. As usual, Sudan was the killer. I was dressed as a Hindu, primed to go, when the wardrobe lady piped up, "Your sandals look too new."

"Dear lady, I am thirty feet from the camera. A lion knocks me down and eats my ribs. If the audience notices the shine on my sandals, we are doing something wrong anyway."

The director agreed with me, and I died with my shiny sandals on.

He did 14 hits on Reggie and 8 on me

Full speed run, all four feet in the air

As in *Cave Bear*, we had an animatronic creation by the best, Stan Winston. A huge lion head with moving eyes and snapping jaws. According to rumor control, Stan charged $3 million for his work, but it wasn't worth three dollars. The management tried to con themselves into accepting the monstrosity, but after a few test shots reality struck home. The six-man animatronic team and their bad actor stuffed head was sent home. Stan Winston was not quite right. His creatures cannot do everything a live animal can. They just cost a lot more.

On January 28, the production company was locked out of the game park for not paying their bills. Fifteen soldiers with submachine guns stand at the gate. The production company threatens to sue the local contacts for misrepresenting South African conditions and luring production to South Africa. Well, that is what happens when you listen to enthusiastic locals.

The film's toughest problem was to make the lions into monsters the audience could hate. In *Jaws*, this was easy. The black, unmoving, soulless eye of a shark guarantees instant fear and hatred. Lions are sometimes feared but mostly respected and admired. Their forward-looking gaze has even a touch of human in it. I suggested lifting a page from *Frankenstein*. The monster is sad and pitiful until he kills the little girl who offers flowers to him. There is nothing more adorable than an African toddler. Let one of the lions menace and stalk one of them and the public will cheer for the hunters. Not surprisingly, my idea was firmly rejected. Instead, the phony lion head chewed a rubber coolie to pieces, but do not look for it on screen. It ended up on the cutting room floor.

The film opened promisingly, but only for one week, then it died. My personal regret is that, because of this half-assed attempt, the most exiting true story of old Africa will never be seen on the screen. There are still two worthy African adventures that should be translated into pictures. Number one, the love story of Martin and Osa Johnson, the original nature filmmakers of the 1920s and '30s. Number two is also a love story, already in a book, *From Cape to Cairo* by Ewart Grogan. Grogan was a ne'er-do-well in the late nineteenth century. He fell in love with a high society English lass, but her father said to him, "You are nothing now and will be the same tomorrow and the rest of your life."

"I'll show you," answered Ewart and, with his faithful gun bearer, walked from Cape Town to Cairo.

In the Sudan, they met a locomotive. Two burning eyes bearing down on them in the twilight. The gun bearer handed him the double-barreled elephant gun. "Here, bwana, shoot the beast." Ewart won his lady's heart, and they lived happily in Kenya until 1964. Here you are, Mr. Producers, two stories in the public domain; just don't let Mr. Goldman write the script. I'd do a better job and certainly cheaper.

CHAPTER 25

ANGKOR WATT, BUT WHAT FOR? OR TIGER, TIGER BURNING BRIGHT

I was seriously contemplating retirement. Forty-five years of wrestling lions, tigers, bears, and producers should be enough for anybody. Then the phone rang. Thierry Le Portier from Paris. "Would you like to work on a film, *The Two Brothers*? It is all about tigers, to be filmed in Cambodia." I signed on. What a chance to see the mystical ruins of Angkor Watt. The director, Jean-Jacques Annaud, created *The Name of the Rose*, *The Bear*, and *Quest for Fire*.

The bad news is that Angkor Watt is in Cambodia, the home of Pol Pot and the killing fields. I flew to France to meet Thierry and to take the script apart. We agreed that if the world did not hate animal trainers before, it surely would after the premiere of *Two Brothers*. It is a cartoon with live animals, and we are giving a helping hand to our own vilification. Well, it is a job. The reps of the National

Geographic Society will be on the set supervising. I wonder what they'll say about anthropomorphizing the striped jungle cat. They'll probably shake their heads, collect their per-diem, and say: "Well, it is a job."

In the rest of this chapter, I'll use excerpts from my diary:

At the Bangkok airport, humid heat wraps around me like the barber's hot towel.

A short flight to Siem Reap on a Russian Antonov 24, complete with a Russian pilot. In midair, smoke started to roll into the cabin in thick waves, but the smiling stew explained it is only fog, normal for an Antonov.

Our group of trainers: Thierry in charge. His number one assistant, Monique Angeon, from the island of Trinidad. I worked with her in South Africa, and she is a delight. Tough, pretty, and loyal. Randy Miller and his two tigers, Shir Khan and Tara, are from California. An interesting addition to our group is Mon Ami Jacques. He is the caretaker and feeder of our thirty-four tigers. Jacques, in his previous life, was a sniper in Vietnam, a truck driver in Columbia [sic], and a mercenary in the Congo. He knows several silent and noisy ways of dispatching humans, and this gives his five-foot-five frame a quiet dignity.

Angkor Watt is a gigantic human achievement only religion or war can create, but after seeing two thousand smiling Buddhas, the two thousand and one loses some of its novelty.

All our locations have something unique about them, like the former headquarters of the Khmer Rouge. It was recently de-mined, but the experts will not sign papers guaranteeing its safety. Red warnings blaze on trees. "Do not leave path or follow a native!" How far he should walk ahead is up to you. At a river location, there are 900 year old carvings in the water. Hundreds of Lingams and Yonis, male and female organs, carved in rock. The Yoni always faces the flow of the water. The Lingam is the representation of the God Kings. I suppose those kings did not mind being called a Big Dick.

Monique filled me in on the behavior of the tigers. Indra is reliable once she knows what is wanted of her, but if she breaks she does it suddenly. If you stand in her way, she'll knock you down but will not hurt you. Taiga is very steady, but if she knocks you down she'll take a bite as well. Prince, Shangan, and Siam should be faced all the time. Turn your back on them, and you might as well call for an ambulance.

Important scene. Mother tiger carrying cub to safety. Instead of a robotic cub, the French used a plush toy. Taiga did several takes to the director's satisfaction, and she was sent back to the compound. The director changed his mind: "I need one more take." Thierry told Jean-Jacques that without Taiga the chances of success are one in a million. "Would you please try?" the director pleads.

Thierry agrees. A trainer hates to say no. Shir Khan, the big American male, is the only possibility. I might add that this is not a trained behavior, not even with Taiga. The tiger grabs the soft inviting toy and steals it. In the receiving cage, after a short while, he gets tired and drops it. The light is rapidly fading. Randy releases Shir Khan. He grabs the plush toy, but instead of moving in the right direction he hunkers down and tears it to bits. Not a very good situation.

When the three of us approach it, he picks up his "prey" and runs into the thick bush. Randy decides to give him a squirt of pepper spray. It works instantly, on the trainers as well. I gag my way through the acrid fog, grab the dummy, and retreat. The crew outside the protective fence heard a lot of noises, tiger and trainer coughing, but no damage was done.

I noticed that our Khmer helpers call all trainers by the same name that sounds something like "komponchat nyat." I asked the interpreter why that is, and she said, "It means those who stand outside the cage." The rest of the crew are in a protective enclosure every time a cat is turned loose. At least they don't call us the fools who run after tigers in 120-degree heat.

November 11. The day of Disney-like footage; in fact, if Walt were still alive, he'd kill for the stuff we got. Taiga and Indra lie on a white sandy beach. The cubs join them, pestering the adults. Indra is patience herself as the little bundles of joy climb all over her. For the final touch, six butterflies hover over her head. In the next scene she'll be shot by the hunter. After this tenderness, there will be no dry seat in the theater.

This is a land of no breezes. The air stands still and hot like fresh plum jam in the cauldron. Luckily, this film is not in "smelevision." Many countries have an individual scent, like wood smoke and mimosa blossoms in Kenya or the spicy breath of sage in California. This country's lingering smell is dried fish and human waste. Sort of eau de poisson and merde, to flaunt my French.

We are moving to a new mountain location near the village of Mondul Keri, five kilometers from the border of Vietnam. The Ho Chi Minh trail runs through it, dotted by grown over American bomb craters. The camp is white canvas tents, like something out of *M*A*S*H*. The door can be closed from the outside only with Velcro. No fly sheet to keep the heat out. A far cry from our romantic African camps, but we are still better off than the company drivers. Usually they stay at a friendly pagoda, but Mondul Keri has no such house of God. They pay $5 to stay in a paper shack, exactly their daily wages. If they insist on eating, the day ends with a slight deficit. "Oh, for the good old days of Pol Pot," I overheard one of them say.

Our leading man, Guy Pearce, had a bit of excitement today. Famis, the cheater, jumped on the protective cage where actor, director, and camera man huddled. Famis is the one that lies with behavior. She'll chuff in the friendliest manner, but if you let her past the advised ten feet, she'll nail you.

I thought I could go through this production without a single enemy, but the Canadian sound man's constant anti-American tirades rub me raw. He is not important enough to be an enemy, just irritating, like yesterday's mosquito bite. The bar and beer hall is in the middle of camp. For the French crew, 10 p.m. is late afternoon, and the boys were really whooping it up with pulsating rap and risqué Gallic songs. The socialist Canadian lives next to this place of merriment, and he is an early sleeper, or would be. He enters indignantly and demands an end to the revelry.

Mon Ami Jacques steps up to him. As I mentioned, Jacques knows several silent and noisy ways to dispatch people. With a flourish, he takes off his glasses and deposits them on the pool table. An obvious warning to the socialist. Next, he steps into the comfort zone of the Canadian and cuts loose with a torrent of words he picked up in the harbors of Oran, Marseilles, and Tobruk. "Atta boy" was not among the words. The complaining sound man turned white like the canvas of his tent, about-faced, and left silently. Mon Ami Jacques got a loud ovation. The lesson served the insomniac sound man right. Why doesn't he use ear plugs like I do?

March 6. Today we worked for our money. Location one hour from *M*A*S*H* camp. The scene: two tigers chasing the butcher's truck. This is the day for the American tigers, Shir Khan and Tara, to shine. We used the electric lure with a slight improvement, Thierry's idea. A bamboo bar attached to the string and, on the bar, two half chickens. Hopefully, both tigers will be rewarded at the end of the run.

Thierry and I are the releasers. The ancient truck rumbles by, the string snaps taut, and the half chickens start their last journey. Shir Khan is in the lead at a fast clip. Not so Tara. "Screw the chicken," she says. "I'd rather eat a sandbag today, the one that holds the microphone." She picks up the heavy double bag like a pointer would a quail. Part of the microphone and the sound cable follow.

She settles down in a weed-choked ditch near the road. Randy is busy with Shir Khan so I stand guard by her while she kills the sandbag. Shir Khan is put up. Randy arrives and squirts Tara with a dose of pepper spray. She releases the bag and melts into the scratchy underbrush. As we follow, we get a dose of the lingering pepper spray. Cough, sneeze, and heavy cussing. Tara is lying quiet as a mouse under a bush. She takes the bait and is leashed up.

Take two. At the moment of release, Shir Khan turns his ass to the door, stuck like a bad racehorse at the starting gate. Take three looks good at the beginning. Both tigers follow the lure, which pulls to the right and brushes against the tripod. Thierry warned the camera crew not to set the machine in the line of the run, but the answer was that is the only spot. So there. The spindly legs tremble and, in slow motion, the camera hits the red dust. The telephoto is attached to the body at an unhealthy angle, like the broken neck of a long-legged wading bird. Somehow the lure gets free and the tigers chase it to the finish. Aside from the broken lens, worth about $250,000, the day is a success. Wrap.

March 7. A day of failure. The temperature is 52 degrees Celsius. I have to look it up in Fahrenheit. It is probably off the scale. We always ask for early morning filming with running shots. They always promise, but it never happens. Take one starts at twenty minutes to noon. If it gets any hotter, both men and beasts will melt.

Take one. I pop Tara's door. She bolts with speed, but Shir Khan's door is stuck. Take two. Both cats leave in good time, but the lure tangles on a clump of grass. Take three and four is a repeat failure. Tara gets her reward; Shir Khan gets zip but comes back to his cage without fuss. On take five, the lure travels at the right speed and direction. Tara follows, but Shir Khan gives up and lies down in the shade. Obviously, we conditioned him to getting his reward on return.

At lunch, I ask for a piece of bread from the director's table. His wife remarks, "You can have a loaf if you guarantee the shot after lunch." I drop the bun. "I can only guarantee that we shall try like a son of a bitch." My standard answer to such requests.

After lunch, one more desperate try. Shir Khan doesn't even leave his cage. On the ninety-first day of shooting, we failed to deliver. At dinnertime, Jean-Jacques drops by our table and gives us a royal bollocking. His target is the absent Thierry, but poor Randy gets plenty of flack.

"It stuns the mind," he fumes. "You guys have time to go to the red house"— he means bordello—"stay up most nights drinking till dawn, and as usual, the head trainer was late this morning. He is preoccupied with his wedding."

I am a clock watcher. We arrived at 7:30. The first take happened at 11:40. How could we be late?

Jean-Jacques blows more smoke. "When I see behavior like this, I think, are these really competent professionals, or am I dealing with rank amateurs?"

At the next table, Guy Pearce is shaking his head and rolls his eyes. He is on our side. Randy is deeply offended. He offers to quit. I resent being called nonprofessional. After ninety successful days, one failure and bingo! We are rank amateurs. An occasional failure is built into this business. Jean-Jacques' last three films were financial disasters. Does that make him an amateur? Monique is mad as a constipated wildcat. She calls Thierry on his way to his wedding. He wanted to turn back but did not.

January 15. Back to Phnom Penh. For ten hours, the minibus jumped from pothole to dust trap, and the driver's skill was directly wired to his horn. He is trying to play a tune, but Hayden's horn concerto it is not. We have two short segments to film here. On the weekend, I visit the infamous killing fields near the capital.

This place is a monument to man's cruelty to his own kind. In the center stands a pagoda three stories high, with glass walls. Through the glass, a multitude of skulls, sorted by age and sex, glisten in the burning sun. Our guide casually reaches behind the wall and takes out a skull with a gaping hole behind the ear. She was killed with a bamboo pole. A skull with a ten-inch cut, the mark of a bush knife. The ground around the pagoda is pockmarked with pits of excavated mass graves. The paths connecting the graves are also studded with human bones. A tibia reaching out of the clay, like a yellow exclamation mark accusing its killers. A jaw bone showing worn teeth of an old person. The scorching wind whistling through the socket of a half exposed skull.

Centuries-old fig tree. Under it, a clay urn full of brittle bones of children. They did not merit a bullet, just a brutal swing against the trunk. I cannot stay any longer. Dazed, I get into a taxi, and at the hotel I fall into a nightmare-ridden sleep.

One more segment to film in Cambodia before we move to Thailand and an air-conditioned sound stage. I keep telling my friends we should have done this show on Stage 15 at MGM. If they could build the Carpathians for *Dracula*, they could surely recreate Angkor Watt. Maybe so, but I admit that even on Stage 15 a forest fire of mega size could not be done. Our special effects crew decided to burn half of Cambodia.

The story says the village folks got tired of the lurking tigers and set the forest ablaze. The circus-educated brother jumps through the flames from boulder to boulder, showing his softer sibling the way out. I was posted behind a papier-mache rock, two tigers running toward me and safety. I made up my mind if the tree five feet behind me catches fire, I get up and run and to hell with the shot, but the tree did not go up in flames.

No one was hurt in the inferno, but the day did not end without accident. A careless porter stuck his finger into Famis the cheater's cage. With one quick bite, she severed the offered digit. She spat it out instantly with distaste. At least we know she is not a man-eater, and the porter is very proud of his bandage.

A Thai actress made a careless slip on a Bangkok TV show. "Angkor Watt belongs to Thailand. The Cambodians stole it from us." In Phnom Penh, an angry mob burned the Thai embassy and several Thai-owned businesses. Not the best time to be in the capital, but I don't think I look Thai. In the meantime,

"Enjoy this beautiful country and its friendly people." This encouraging sentence is written on every call sheet we get.

Not all the romance of my friends happened on a pay-as-you-go basis. True love also raised its beautiful head. Our boss, Thierry, fell lock, stock, and barrel for a gorgeous, traditional Apsara dancer. She looks like one of the carvings on the temple wall in Angkor. Of course, she is a virgin and will stay so till the wedding night.

We are all invited to the festivities. It starts with four hours of kneeling while the monk in a saffron robe chants his blessings. Seven changes of costume for the groom, and only Buddha knows how many for the bride. Thierry, the man who backs off to no tiger, looks dazed and bewildered. I can surely relate to his feelings.

On Monday, an endless photo session at the ruins. Thierry finally puts his foot down. "No more pictures, no more costume changes. I want to be alone with my bride." I am sure we'll hear details later. He already predicted she'll be a volcano. After seven changes of bridal gowns, I certainly hope so, but Thierry was a gentleman. All he told us was that she wore a flannel PJ with teddy bears on it. How charming is that?

For the last stage of this saga, we move to Bangkok. The opulence of the Radisson Hotel feels heavenly after the dusty, nomadic existence at the *M*A*S*H* camp at Mondul Keri. In a warehouse, a large part of Angkor has been recreated. It looks better than the original and a lot cooler, even if the AC works only part of the time. Despite "No Smoking" signs all over, the crew smokes like Russians. The poor assistant director says, "What can I do? The director's wife smokes." Well, that makes it okay to Gallic minds and discipline.

April 12. Thai New Year.

We all donned loud Hawaiian shirts and were squirted all day with water. Monique did not find it very funny. Her camera got wet, and she wanted to put the offending Thai's head down the loo.

Jean-Jacques left the tiger mating scene to the end. For two days we have been filming tiger balls. The testicles of Shir Khan and Prince loping away from camera. Dangling balls are followed by tigers mating on camera. This French director has the luck of the Irish. Prince and Bondeale got into a passionate hump under the bemused smile of a Buddha statue. Thierry was as pleased with the shot as if he were doing it. Only the French would put sex scenes into a family picture. The American version will have a discreet long shot of Shir Khan and Tara.

April 16, 2003. During filming, one of the fruit bats gave birth in midair. A little pink demon, hanging by an invisible umbilical cord, following the mother.

My Asian escapade has finally come to an end. Now that it is over, I would not trade it for a million, but if I had to start all over, I would not sign on for a million. Jean-Jacques is on the same flight to Paris. He is all smiles. The day of disaster at Mondul Keri is all forgotten but not by me. It lives on the page of my memoirs. Jean-Jacques did one very decent thing. He gave Thierry credit on the movie's poster. This has never happened to a trainer before or after. Well deserved, Thierry.

Dear reader, do not take my complaints too seriously. Angkor Watt is truly a magnificent sight. Go and see it; "Enjoy that beautiful country and its friendly people."

CHAPTER 26

BITS AND PIECES

During my active years, my animals appeared in one hundred fifty features, two hundred TV shows, and many commercials. To report all would make a book larger than the Encyclopedia Britannica. I could not do that to possible readers, but I pick out random bits and pieces.

On *Naked Gun 2 1/2 Half*, Robert Goulet played the guest villain. A stuntman took his high fall, and I doubled him in the lion attack. When the cameras stopped, the three of us stood on a Burbank street all dressed and made up like Mr. Goulet, but only he had the amazing tenor voice. Spontaneously, he burst out in his trademark song: "If ever I should leave you . . ." The two of us joined in. The citizens of Burbank looked at us, shaking their heads.

In *Dr. Dolittle*, there were a few minutes when only Rex Harrison and I were in the scene. Me as a nineteenth-century seal trainer. After the first take, Richard Fleischer, our patient director, summoned me. "I hope the wristwatch you are wearing is a period piece, but take it off anyway."

The Amboseli Park in Kenya with the snow-covered dome of Kilimanjaro is one of the most photographed natural wonders and, until recently, home to prides of lions. Sadly, the Maasai speared most of them. In 1992, Sudan, the best lion that ever lived, played the role of a man-killer very convincingly. At night he was in his traveling home behind the Amboseli Lodge. At two o'clock in the morning, I woke up to lion talk. Not one but two. Grabbing a flashlight, I approached cautiously and witnessed a tender, sad event. One of the last remaining lionesses came to see my California-born lion. She nuzzled up to the wire, and if lions can coo, she did. Sudan reciprocated with gentle murmurs, rubbing against this lonely femme fatale.

Cheeta the cheater. He appeared in *News Week*, *People* magazine, and the prestigious *Los Angeles Times*. He had an agent who would tell anyone her client was seventy-five years old. The oldest-living primate, Johnny Weissmuller's costar in the *Tarzan* movies. His "paintings" sold for $135. Even the "infallible" *Guinness Book of World Records* swallowed the red herring of his longevity. On his birthday, Jane Goodall sang happy birthday to him in chimpaneeze. We are talking about Cheeta the chimp. The former employees of Jungleland are slowly going the way of the dodo bird, but a few of us are still alive and know the truth. The ape creating all this publicity and adoration is a fraud.

In 2007 I got a call from Richard Rosen, a journalist and Edgar Award-winning author. Mr. Rosen was working on a book about this Hollywood has-been, but he had some doubts. I told him I knew Tony Gentry and his ape and agreed to a meeting. The falsehood of all this publicity has bothered me before. I invited two of the former Jungleland trainers, Cheryl Shawver and Stuart Rafill, for this truth-hunting session. We told Mr. Rosen that Wally Ross was manager of Pacific Ocean Park when it closed in 1967. Among the animals looking for a new home was a chimp named Cheeta. Wally asked, "Tony, you want him?" Tony said yes. The ape, in 1967, was about seven years old.

Tony was an interesting character, more colorful than Joseph's Technicolor Dream Coat. He would entertain us with his past, how he captured wildlife from orangs to rhinos with *Bring Them Back Alive*'s Frank Buck. Filming *Dr. Dolittle* on the Island of St. Lucia, Tony looked up at a shiny satellite gliding through the velvet sky. "Well, you know that I trained for the Air Force, Ham, the first chimp in space." We all took Tony's fables with a big spoonful of salt. Not really believing but not questioning either. He was an entertaining old coot but left the tallest of his tall tales for posterity.

In 1993, an ailing Tony gave Cheeta to his cousin, Dan Westfall. With the chimp, Tony sold Westfall a collection of untruth that is remarkable even in the town that was built on fiction. Hollywood bought the life and legend of Cheeta. The fact is that he never appeared in any movie, never mind a *Tarzan* epic, *Bed Time for Bonzo*, or *Dr. Dolittle*. I was a part of that film from prep to wrap. The role of Chee-Chee was played by an ugly female named Dee-Dee, and Tony did work her.

The time and place vary, but in most interviews Tony said he captured the little simian in Liberia and flew him home on a Pan-Am transatlantic flight. Fact: transatlantic flights were not in service until 1939. A fibber should have a good memory. Tony did not. In a *Los Angeles Time*s article in 1985, Tony said, "I bought him from a dealer when they closed down the Santa Monica Pier. Let me see, when was that? Late '30s sometime. Maybe 1938. He was about 2 or 3 years old . . . so he did one movie with Lex Barker, or was it two with Weissmuller and one with Barker? Which ones? I don't know." In 1985, shortly after the *Los Angeles Times* article, in *People* magazine, Gentry said he pampered and trained Cheeta for thirty-eight years; 1985 minus thirty-eight means Cheeta was born in 1947, or fifteen years later than the original date of 1932. Also, the location has changed from Liberia to the Belgian Congo. Just look at the map of Africa. The two countries are not even near.

According to Mr. Rosen's excellent research, Cheeta was either seventy-five, seventy-two, sixty, or possibly fifty-nine, and then he talked to the three of us, Cheryl, Stuart, and me. Mr. Rosen communicated to Westfall all the facts he found. Westfall replied, "Well, that is what Tony told me." I never met Westfall, but I am fairly certain he is a well-meaning member of the Animal Protection Industry, and from Uncle Tony he inherited a yarn more tangled than the famed Gordian knot.

Westfall was concerned about having sold Cheeta's paintings under false pretenses. He edited his website to read, "Very recently, Dan has been working with an author on Cheeta's biography. The author's research revealed that Cheeta may not be quite as old as we'd thought, although he is clearly old. It has also been difficult to determine which movies our Cheeta may have been in. This will also remain a Hollywood mystery." Even this slight correction was decent of Westfall, but I wonder if he is still asking for $135 donations for his charge's paintings.

A chance encounter, Jackie Kennedy and Arusha

Kibor and Mac, cat friendship

Christmas at the ranch, Doree Hubert, Kibor, Mac, Mushroom, and Siafu

Three days in hell. California is an ideal place to live in about three hundred days of the year. The remaining sixty-five are not quite so pleasant. Earthquakes rumble, mudslides move your house to the next zip code, race riots flare, or hot winds from the desert bring fire. My frisky terrier stops in the middle of the path. His wet nose points at the rock wall of the canyon. Like a mythical sea serpent, a thick brown vortex of smoke is rising against the backdrop of deep blue sky. The same night, the flames chewed a ten-mile-wide swath on the parched back of the mountains. I was at a photo shoot in Hollywood. At noon the phone rang, alarming like the bell of a fire truck. "Return at once; the fire has changed directions, and it is approaching the ranch." I made it home in record time and took the first steps to evacuate. Trucks, trailers, shipping crates all lined up.

At 1:30 p.m., the first blades of fire appear at the western end of the canyon. I load Sudan, then Rahny, my prize tigress, then the wolves are led into trailers. Noah must have felt something similar, but in our case the flood was not the enemy.

At 2:40 p.m., two sheriff's deputies roll in on Harley-Davidsons. Reflecting sunglasses mirror my distorted dusty face. "You must leave now. There are fifteen wildfires around us."

"I realize the situation, but I am staying. Worse comes to worse, I'll jump into my sea-lion pool."

The officers write my name down, unwilling to evacuate, and roll toward the safety of town. The flames are creeping closer. The situation reminded me of 1944 when the Soviet Army crossed the Carpathian Mountains. We knew the red tide would reach us; the question was when?

Four o'clock p.m. The fire reached the middle of the rock wall. There is no sign of firefighters; they are stretched too thin, but President Clinton declared on TV that he is feeling with us. Thanks, Mr. Prez.

Eight p.m. After sunset, the fireworks became more mysterious and menacing. The African masks on my wall dance to the tune of "diabolique."

Eleven p.m. Two huge fire trucks roll into my yard. There is one slight problem. They are from LA County, and their hose coupling does not fit my Ventura County fire plug. "Not to worry," says the young captain, "if we last till morning, the helicopters will fix this little brushfire."

Eight a.m. Help is here. Helicopters, giant humming dragonflies and fixed-wing planes, their pilots risking their lives, lay down a wet carpet on the dry earth. We continue to move the animals to safety. Two mule deer, the rest of the wolves, and my seventy-five African birds.

Twelve-thirty p.m. The wind gained speed. The sheriff returns. Evacuation is now mandatory. From the end of the canyon, growling like a herd of T-Rex, an insane locomotive is bearing down on us. The moment of my last painful duty has arrived. Asali, my wonderful lioness, the companion of four African safaris, is so old she cannot jump into the back of the truck. I cannot leave her to suffer from flames and smoke. Tears plow a furrow on my sooty face. Asali looks at me with confidence. Her amber eyes tame the red menace to the memories of African sunsets. Through my tears, but with firm hand, I pull the trigger. The most beautiful lioness collapses as if hit by lightning. With one more glance, I say goodbye to my home and my memories. In the last sharp turn, a reporter stands in my way. "How do you feel now that . . ." I refuse to answer, and the caravan leaves the canyon. The fire brigade, aided by volunteer convicts, is staying. Shovels on shoulders, they march toward the bottom the valley. I have never seen more sympathetic convicts.

Mark, one of my trainers, puts me up in his guest room. After three days of tension, I cannot sleep. The TV shows the conflagration. A quick shot of Carlisle Canyon. White house with red tiles. My home is still standing. A huge C-47 covers it with a rosy cloud of deterrent.

I cannot stand it anymore. I have to go back. Two miles from my house, firemen stop me. I leave my truck on the roadside and continue on foot. On both sides of the road, red embers wink like the sleepy eyes of a tired dragon. The scenery changed so much it is like a negative deja-vu. I have never been here before. I reach my mailbox. It is untouched. Hope fills me. The white walls greet me with a silent sigh. Searching in the dark, I find a Christmas candle. Its timid flame flickers like the symbol of hope.

Seventy-thirty a.m. Among the scarred bushes, quails are calling for missing mates. New day, new chapter, the beginning of new life.

THE AGE OF STONE LIONS

ran my race, I reached the finish line, and I lived to write about it. Imagination is the most vivid in the early years. Many an hour I spent under the shade of the huge chestnut tree, reading and dreaming about faraway places, but I never dreamed I'd work on all five continents. Antarctica does not count. It is only a slab of frozen mass that fell off the Creator's ice wagon.

Lions don't roar anymore in my garden, but I still have two magnificent stone sentinels guarding my entrance. They are so perfect; they even have personalities. Kibor is on the right, exactly on his mark. Sudan is the kindest but a tad sloppy. His right front paw is off the platform.

The age of the stone lions

The reasons for writing these pages are twofold. Most people are fascinated by filmmaking, and trainers have been part of this machine since *The Birth of a Nation*. I'd like to cast a narrow beam of light on this profession that is either hated or admired but never understood.

Times change. I have not accomplished what my idol, Melvin Koontz, did in the '30s and '40s, and the next generation will not have the opportunity to take four lions, three leopards, an elephant, and a rhino to Kenya like I did. It is not just a figure of speech, but we are an endangered species. CGI, computer-generated images, is one reason, even if leopards look ridiculous, like in *Hidalgo*, or wolves look cheesy, like in the *Twilight Saga*. What hurts me most is that our detractors deny our love for our furry and feathered friends.

To quote from "The Once Again Prince" by Irving Townsend, "We who choose to surround ourselves with lives even more temporary than our own, live within a fragile circle, easily and often breached." Though hard to accept its awful gaps, we still would not live any other way. I still have ambitions. I'd like to see one of my five scripts on the silver screen.

Kwa-Heri is an old-fashioned love story with a very modern twist. Don't try it at home.

The heroine is twenty; he is forty. To even the age gap, he voluntarily undergoes twenty years of cryogenic sleep. When he comes back, they are both forty. Does he get the girl?

Commercially most viable is *Valeria*, a lady vampire, but she is not the run-of-the-mill bloodsucker, and she is in love with a mortal. A violin virtuoso like Paganini, the devil's fiddler.

Just recently, a reporter asked me what I would change if I could start all over. Without hesitation, I replied, "I'd like to be rich," But the truth is, the only variation I'd take is being a big, black-maned lion on the Serengeti plains with a harem of tawny lionesses.

THE END

ABOUT THE AUTHOR

Hubert Geza Wells has trained hundreds of Hollywood actors, but none of them talk about it. The veteran coach doesn't take it too hard—he knows that some movie actors are just animals. And he's never surprised when they try to bite the hand that feeds them. Hungarian-born Wells is one of the movie industry's most respected and enduring animal experts. For the past forty-four years, he has made a living—through his company Animal Actors of Hollywood—by persuading an encyclopedic range of animals to perform for the camera. Wells has trained animals for more than one hundred films, including *Out of Africa, Ring of Bright Water, Born Free, Living Free, Sheena, Lady Hawk,* and *The Ghost and the Darkness.* After having filmed on all five continents, he now devotes his time to writing about his unique experiences in book and script form.

Morgan James
Speakers Group

www.TheMorganJamesSpeakersGroup.com

We connect Morgan James published authors with live and online events and audiences whom will benefit from their expertise.

Printed in the USA
CPSIA information can be obtained
at www.ICGtesting.com
JSHW022220140824
68134JS00018B/1159

9 781683 500995